Beautiful Birds & Pretty Patterns

A Bird Nerd Coloring Book Gift

Firstly, thank you for purchasing this great coloring book. We have spent loads of time making the best illustrations of these beautiful birds for you to enjoy!

You will find some color testing pages at the front of the book, these are to check the pens and pencils you are using so that you don't accidentally ruin your pages.

We hope that you have as much fun using this coloring book as we did making it. Now get going and feel the stress leave your body!

With love, Veich Publishing.

Pigment Testing Page

Pigment Testing Page

Pigment Testing Page

Pigment Testing Page

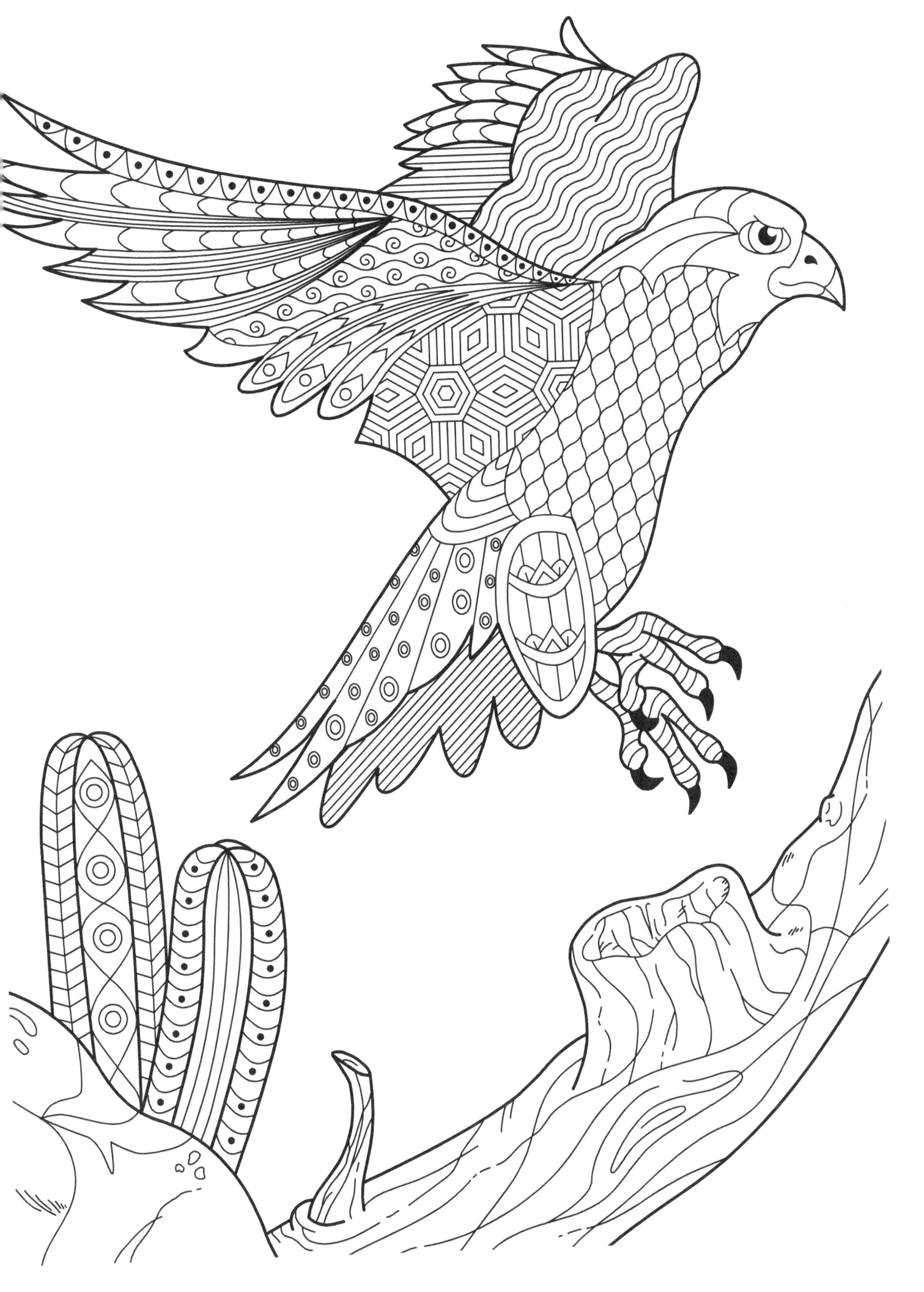

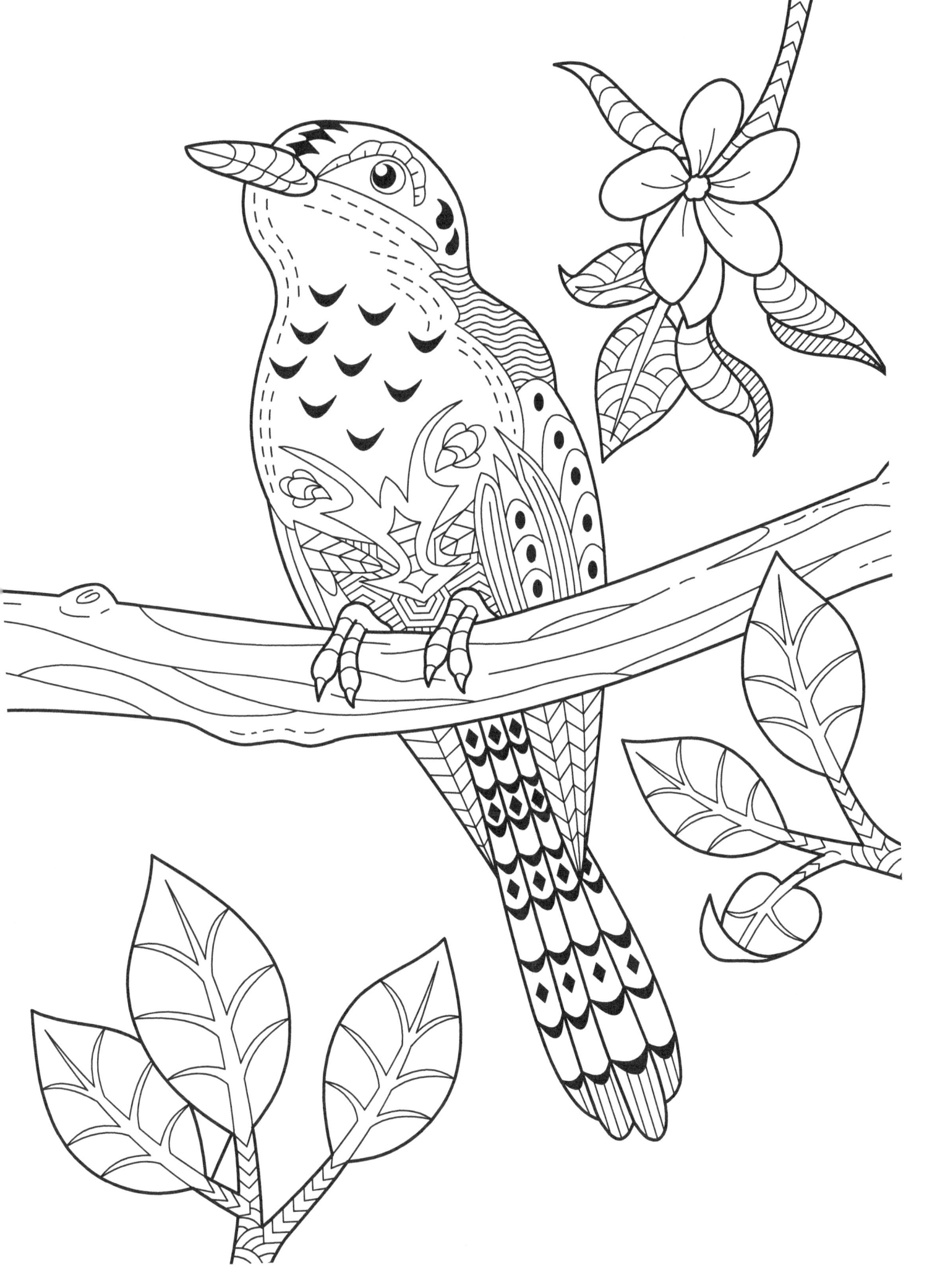

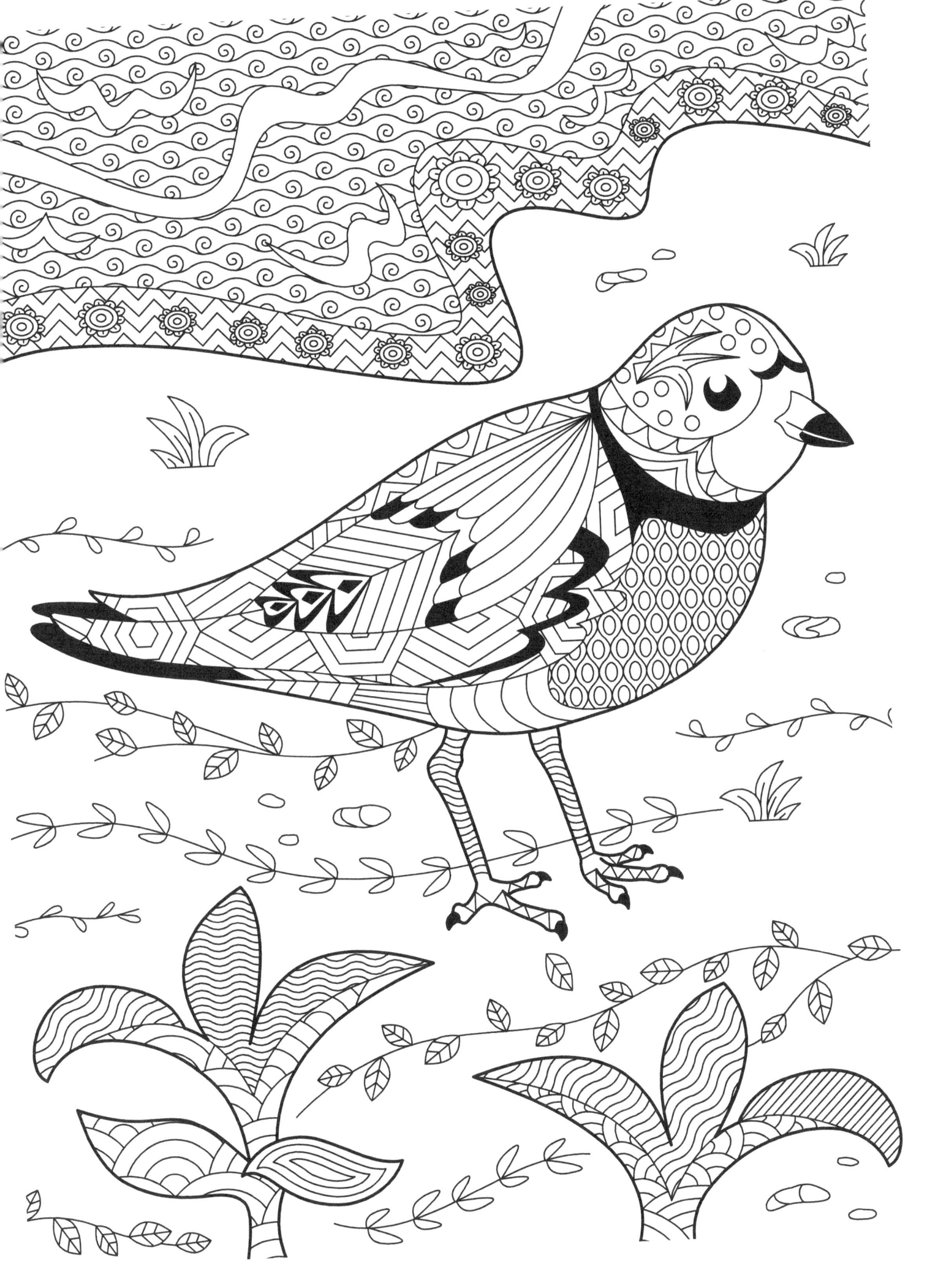

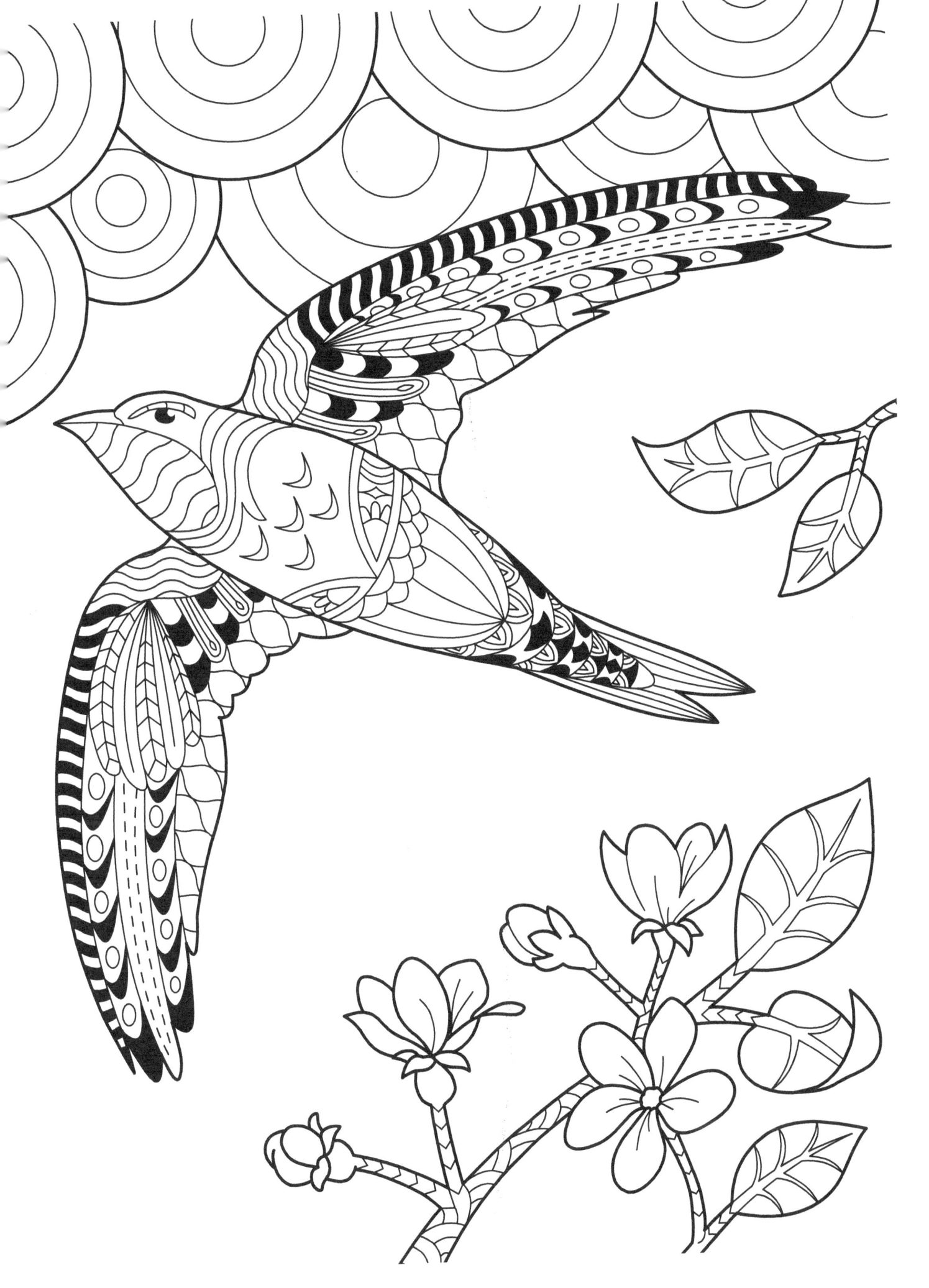

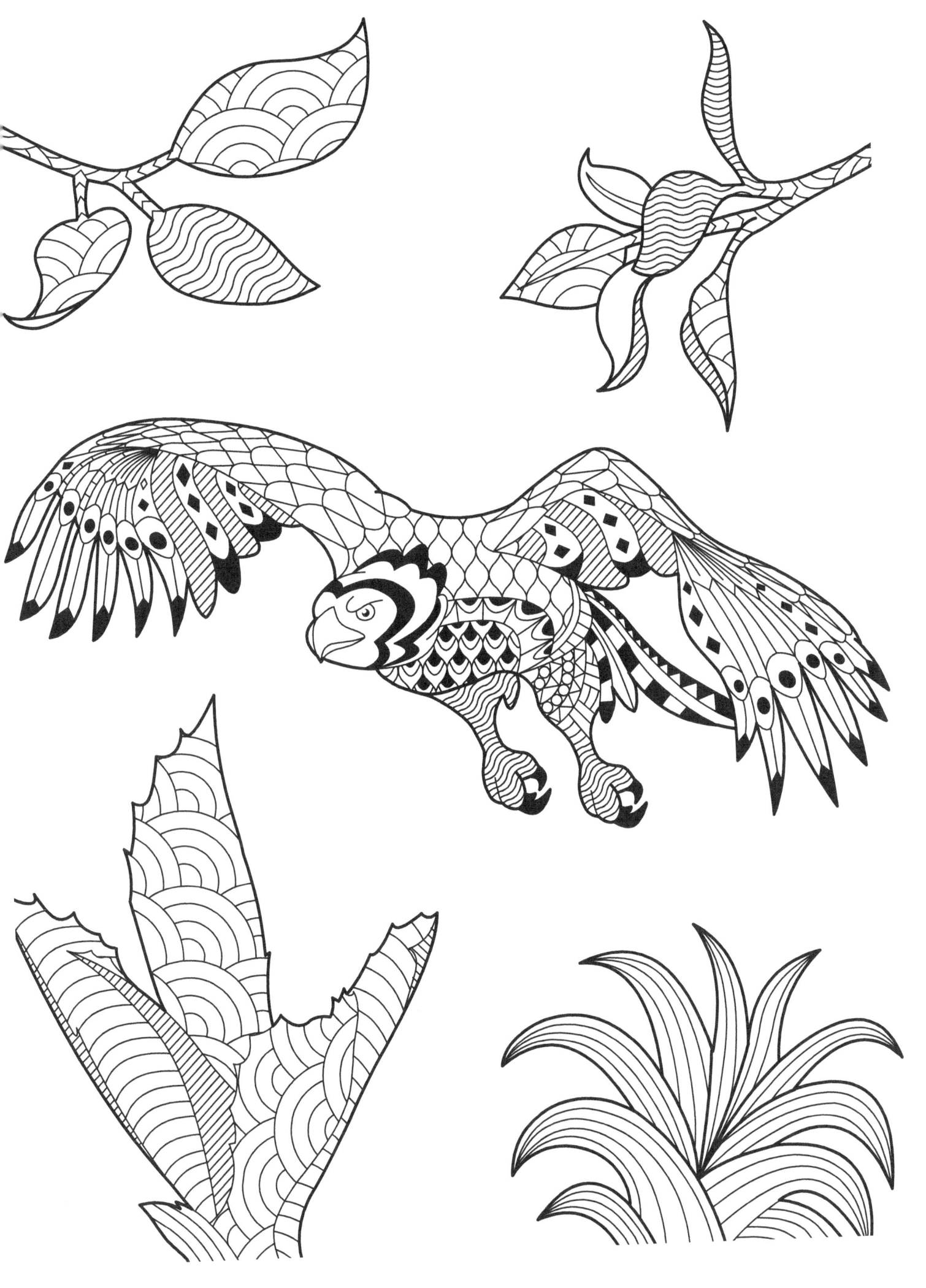

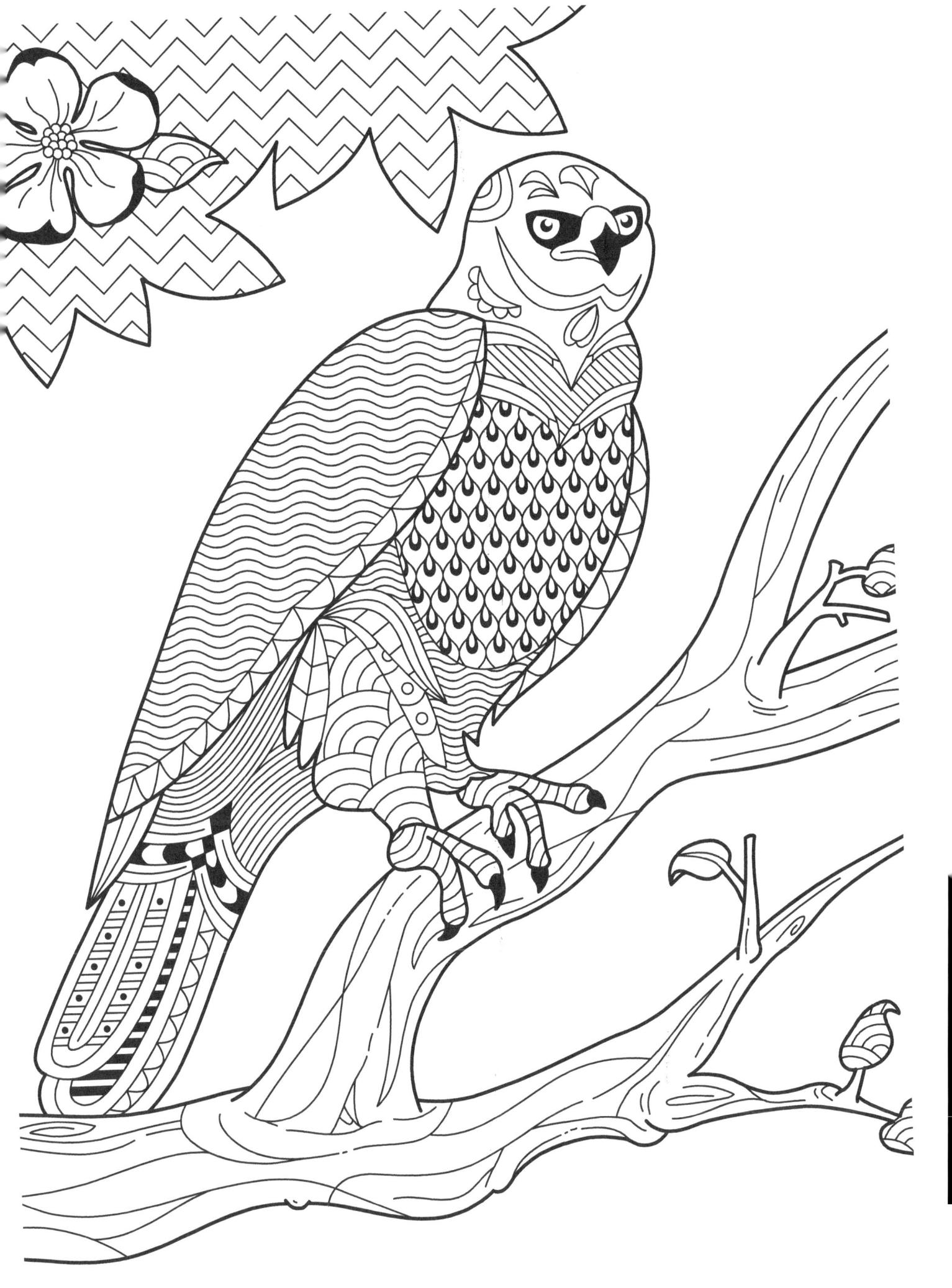

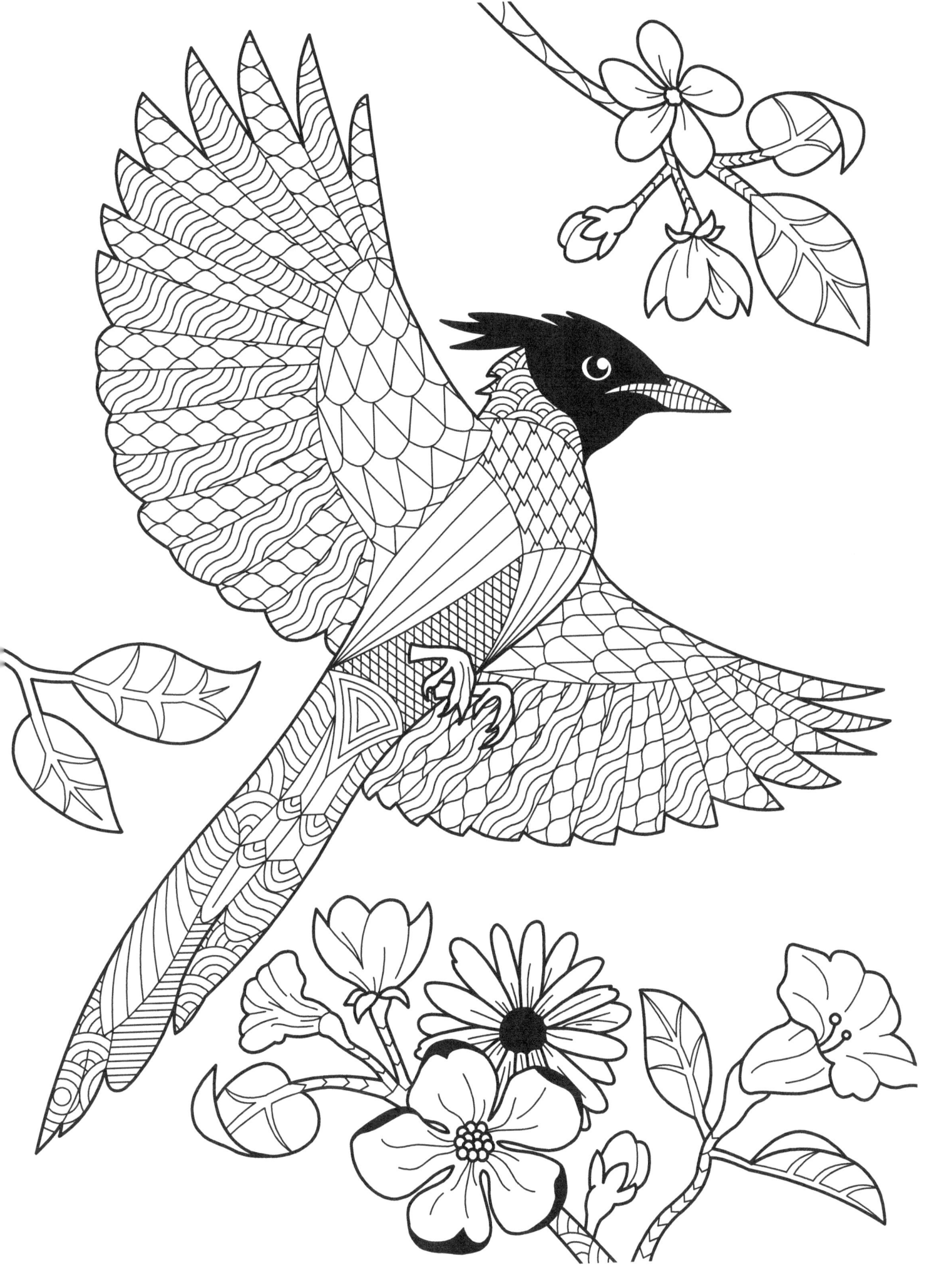

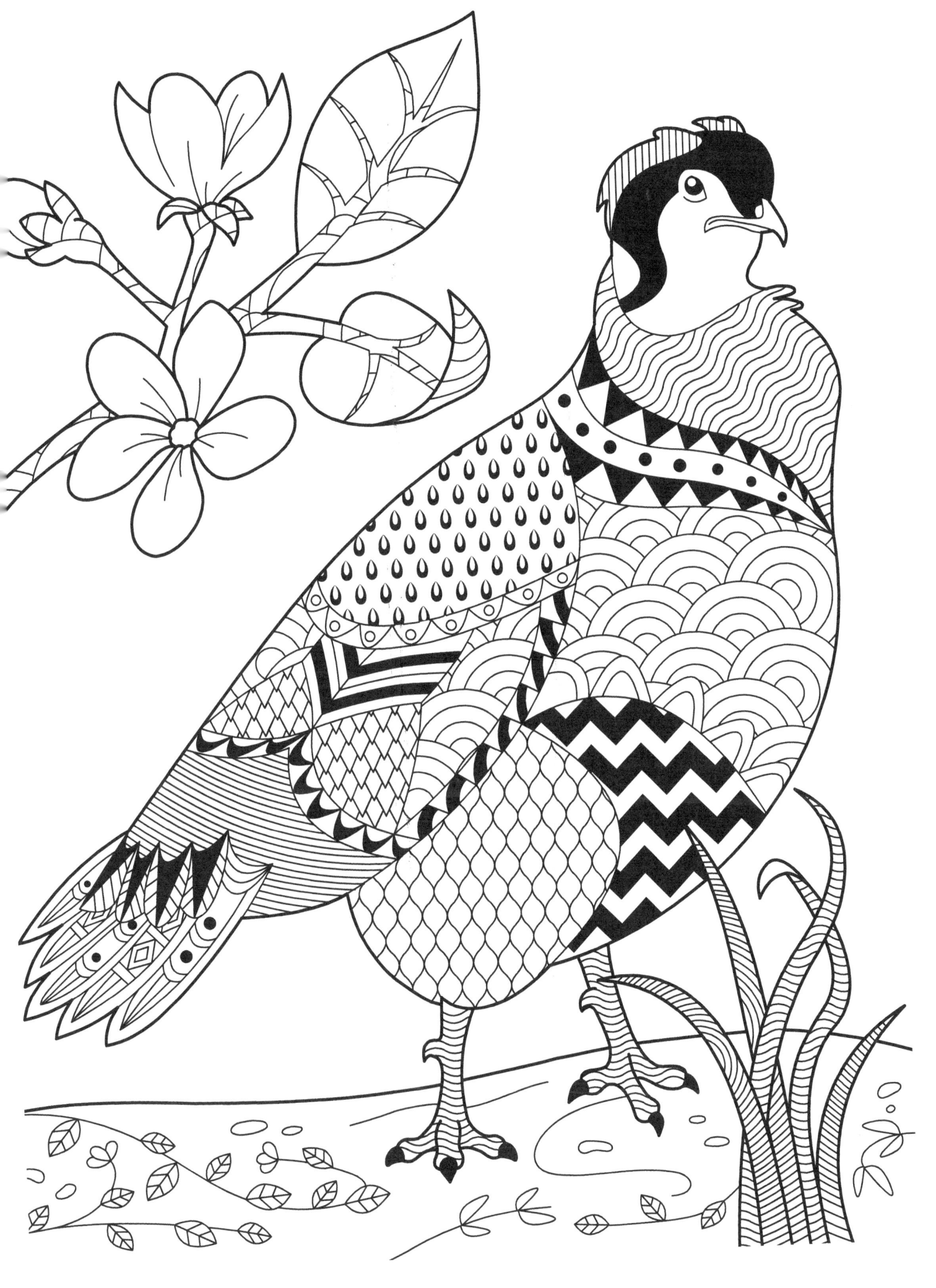

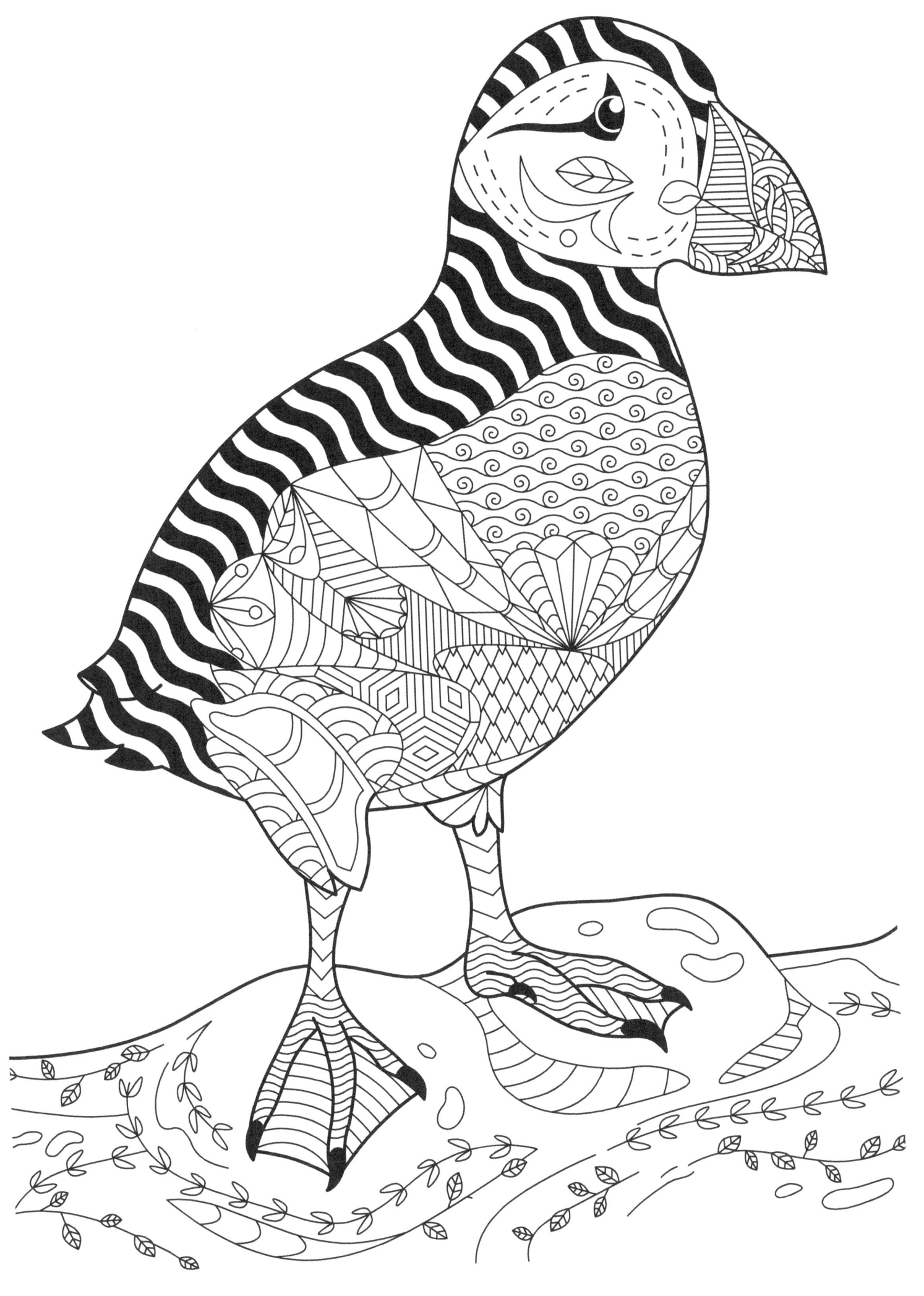

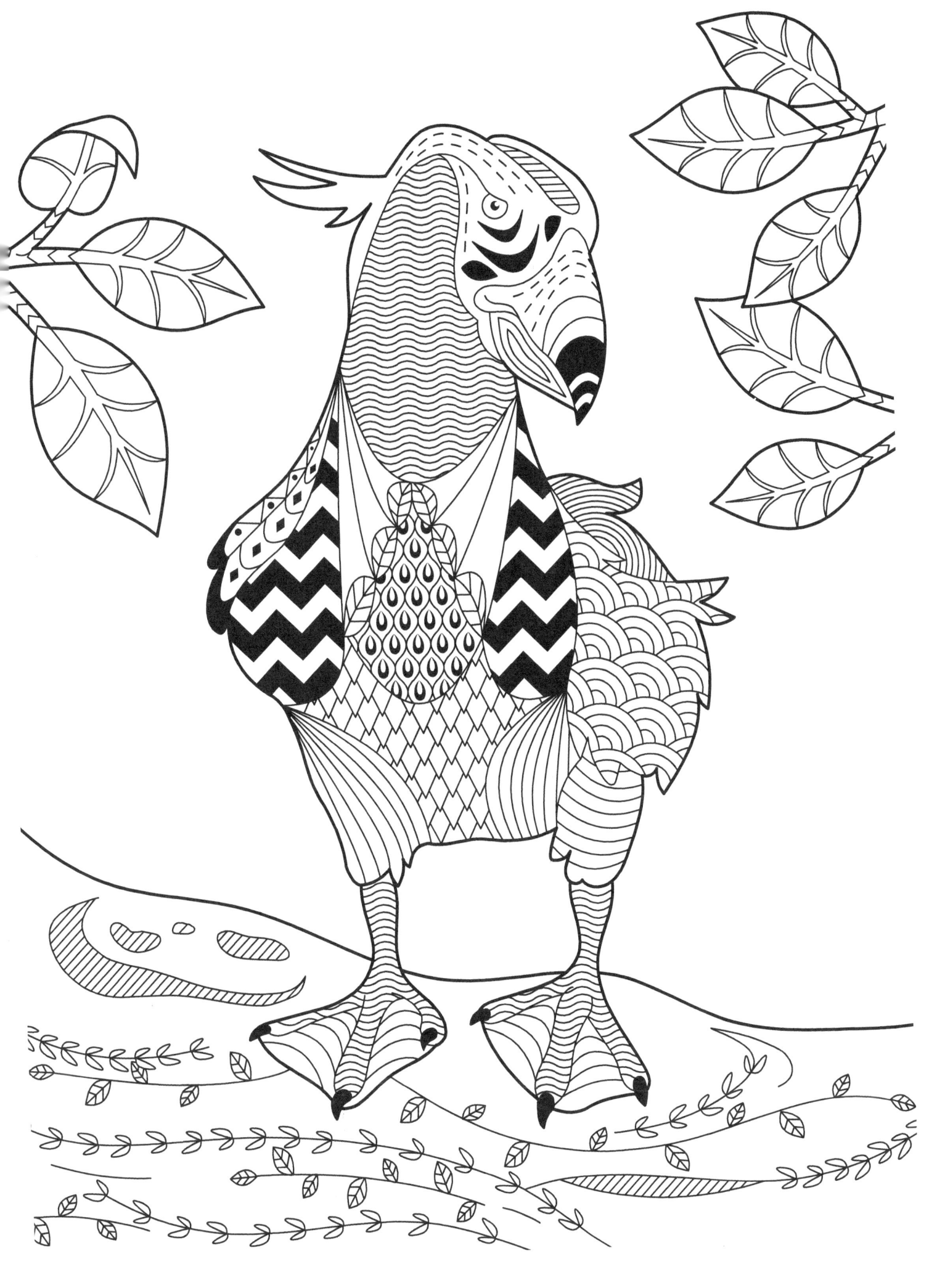

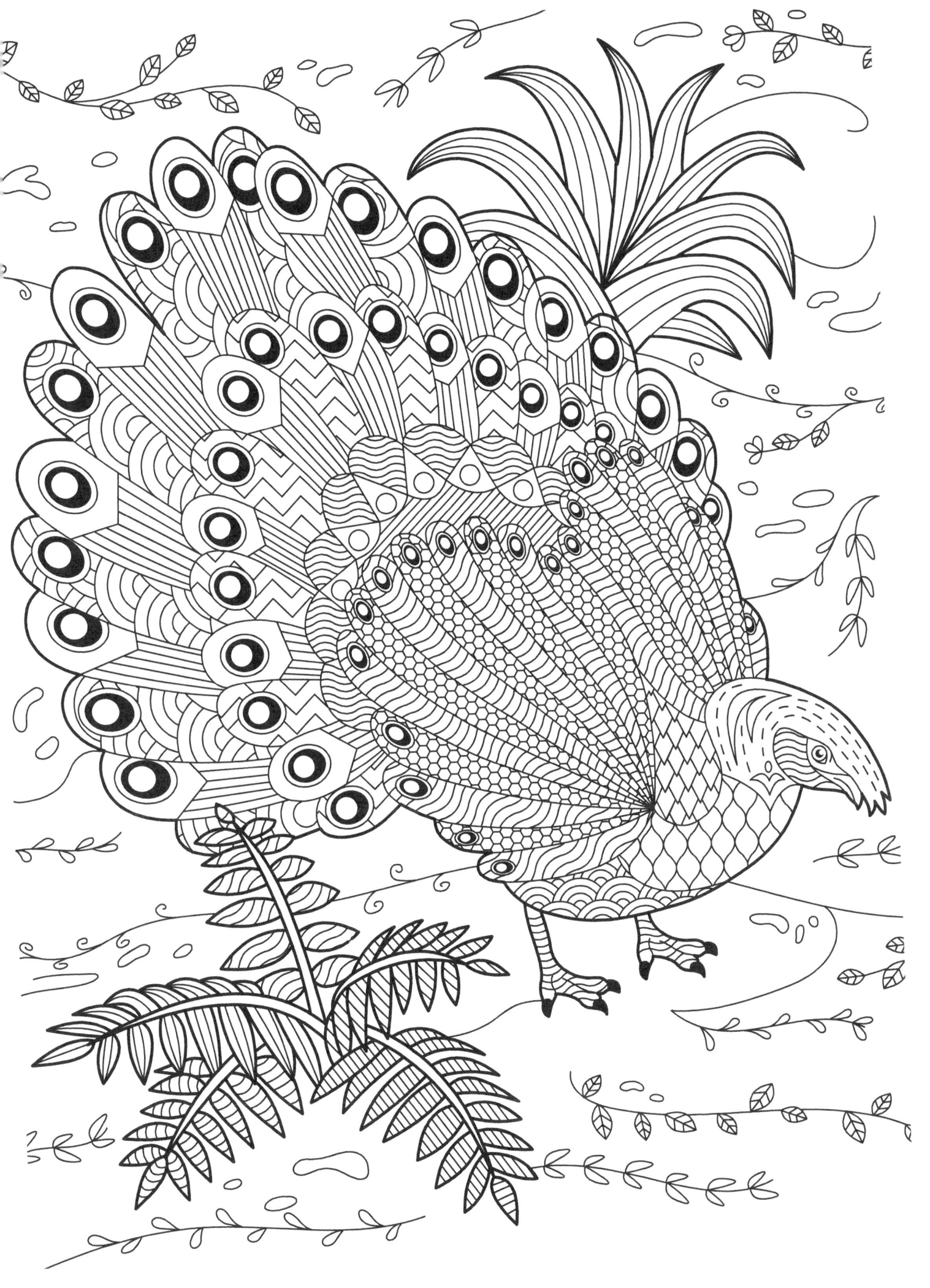

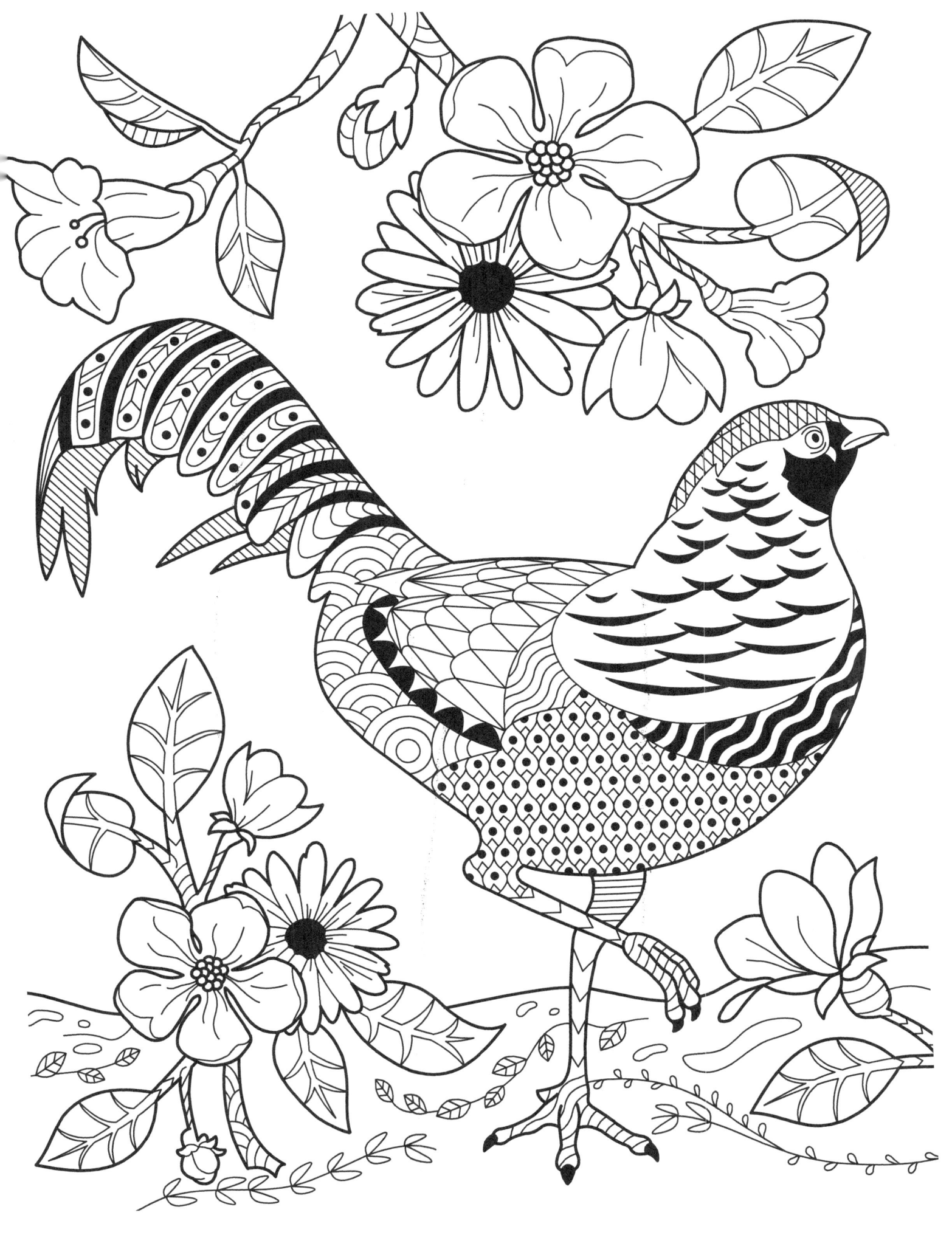

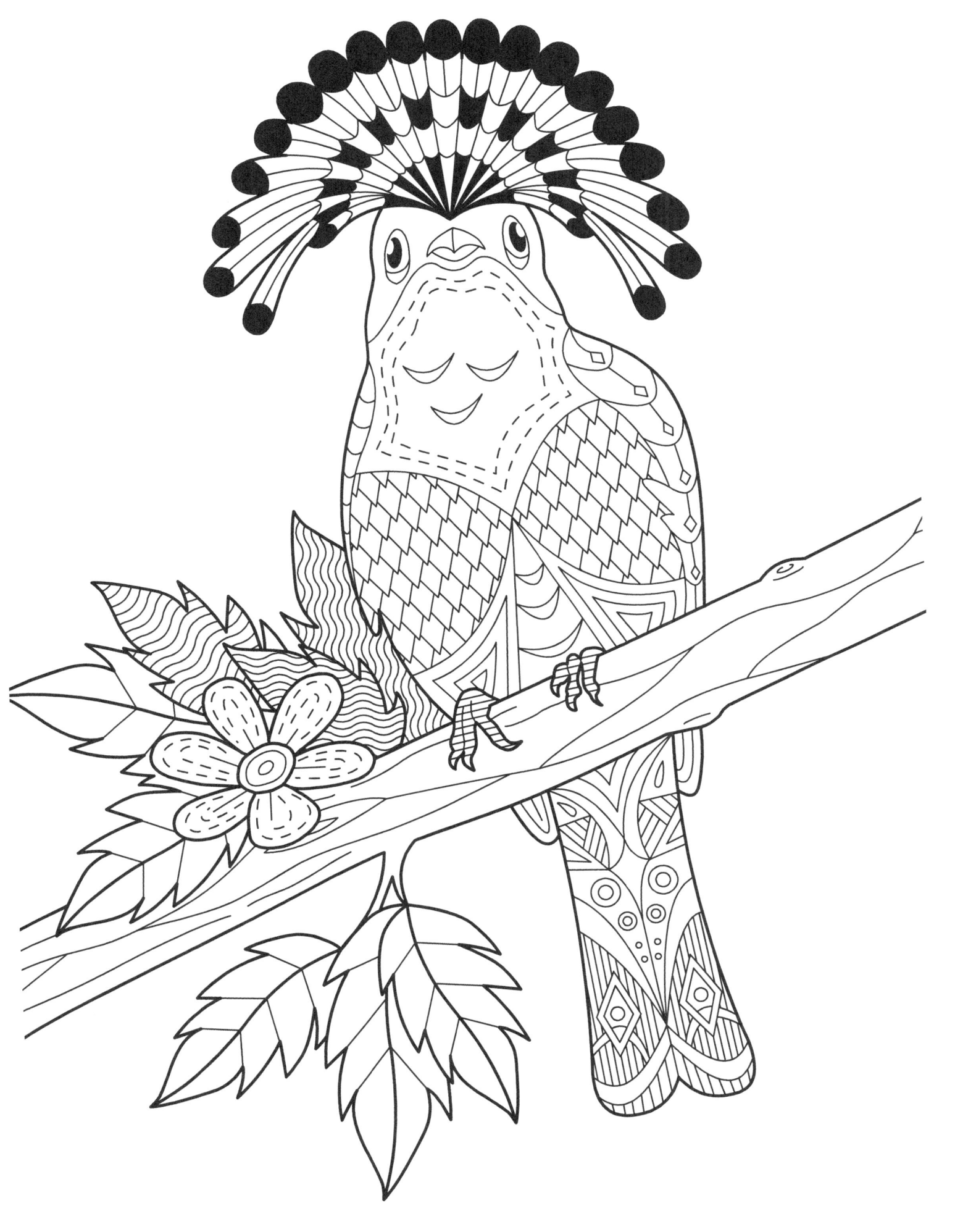

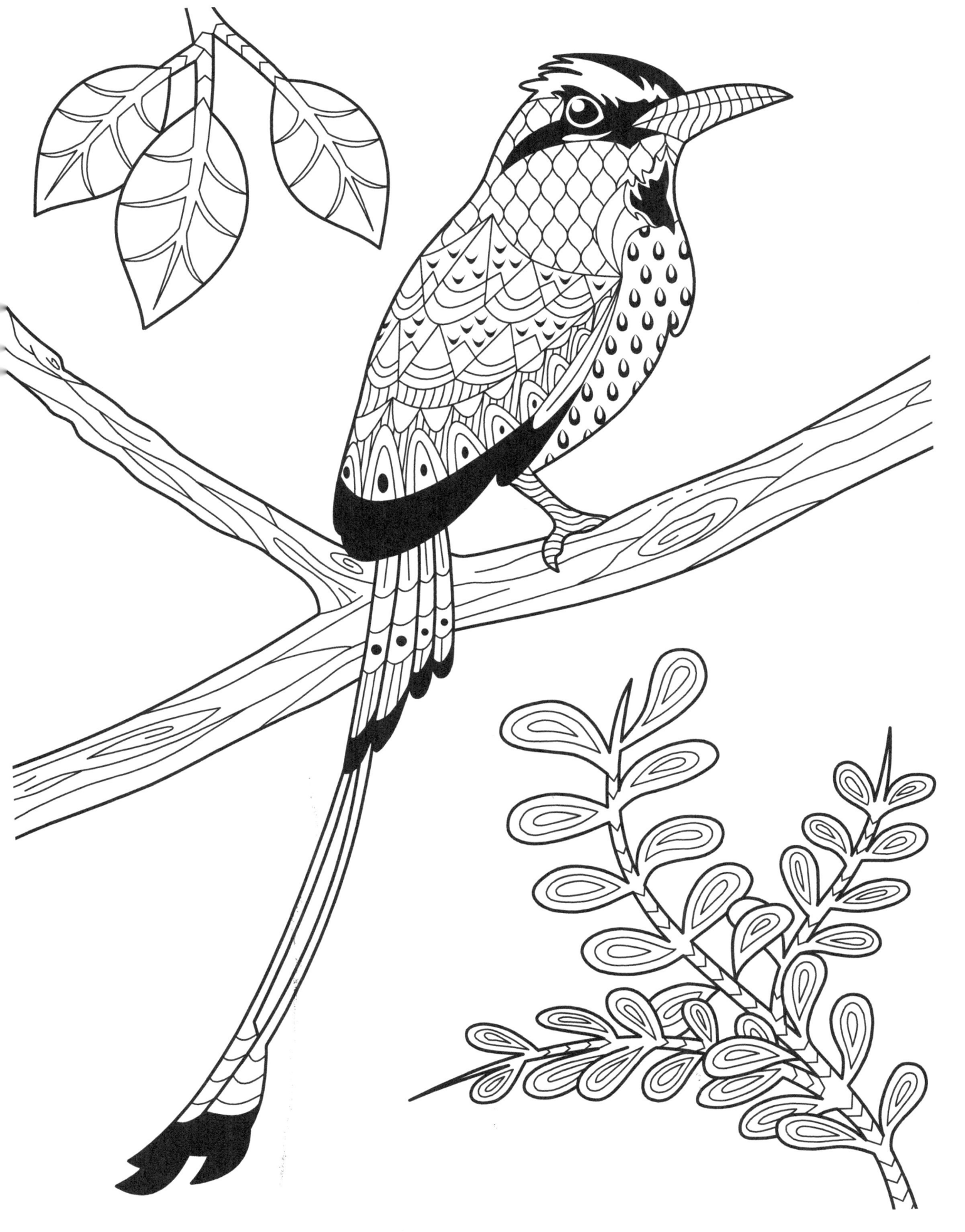

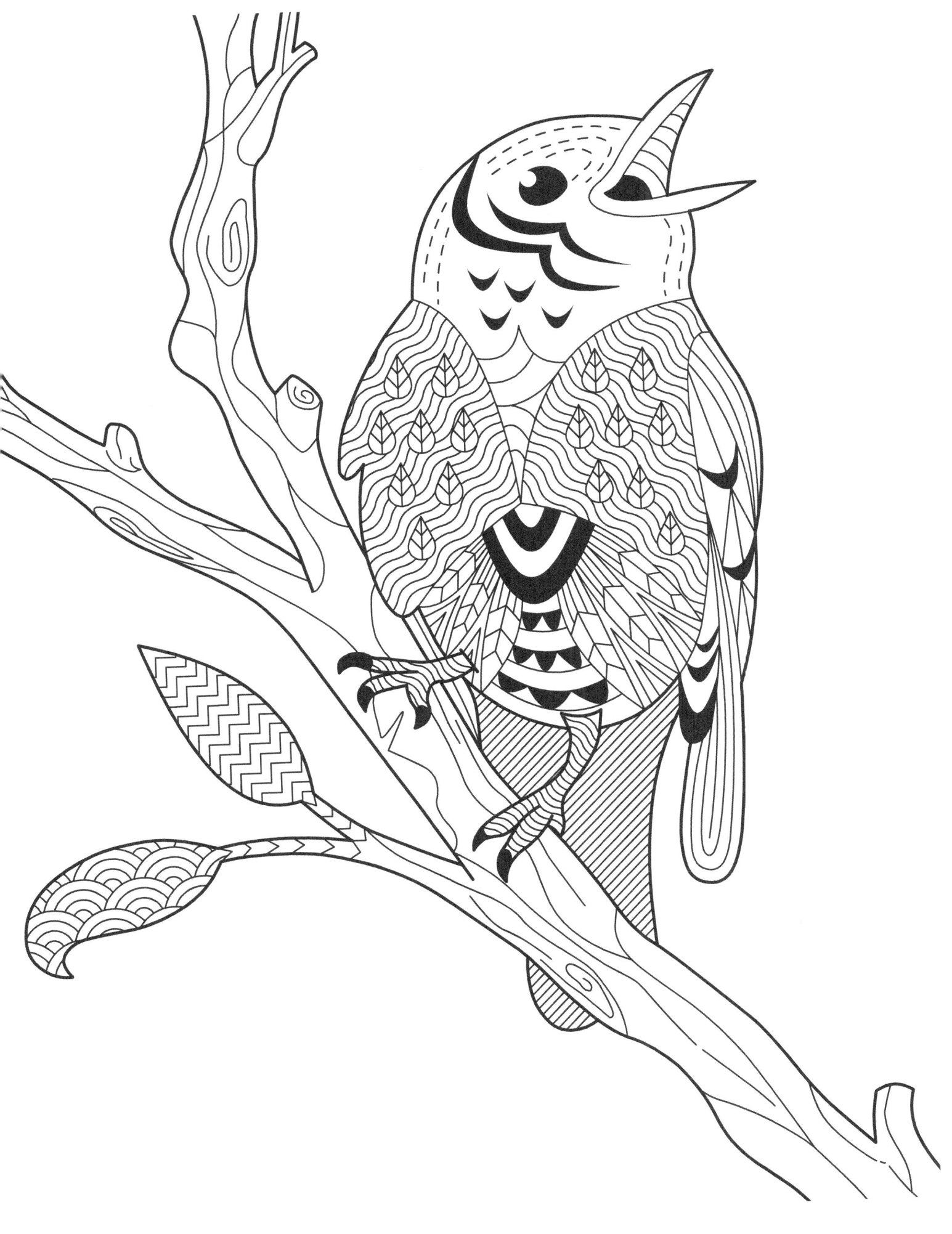

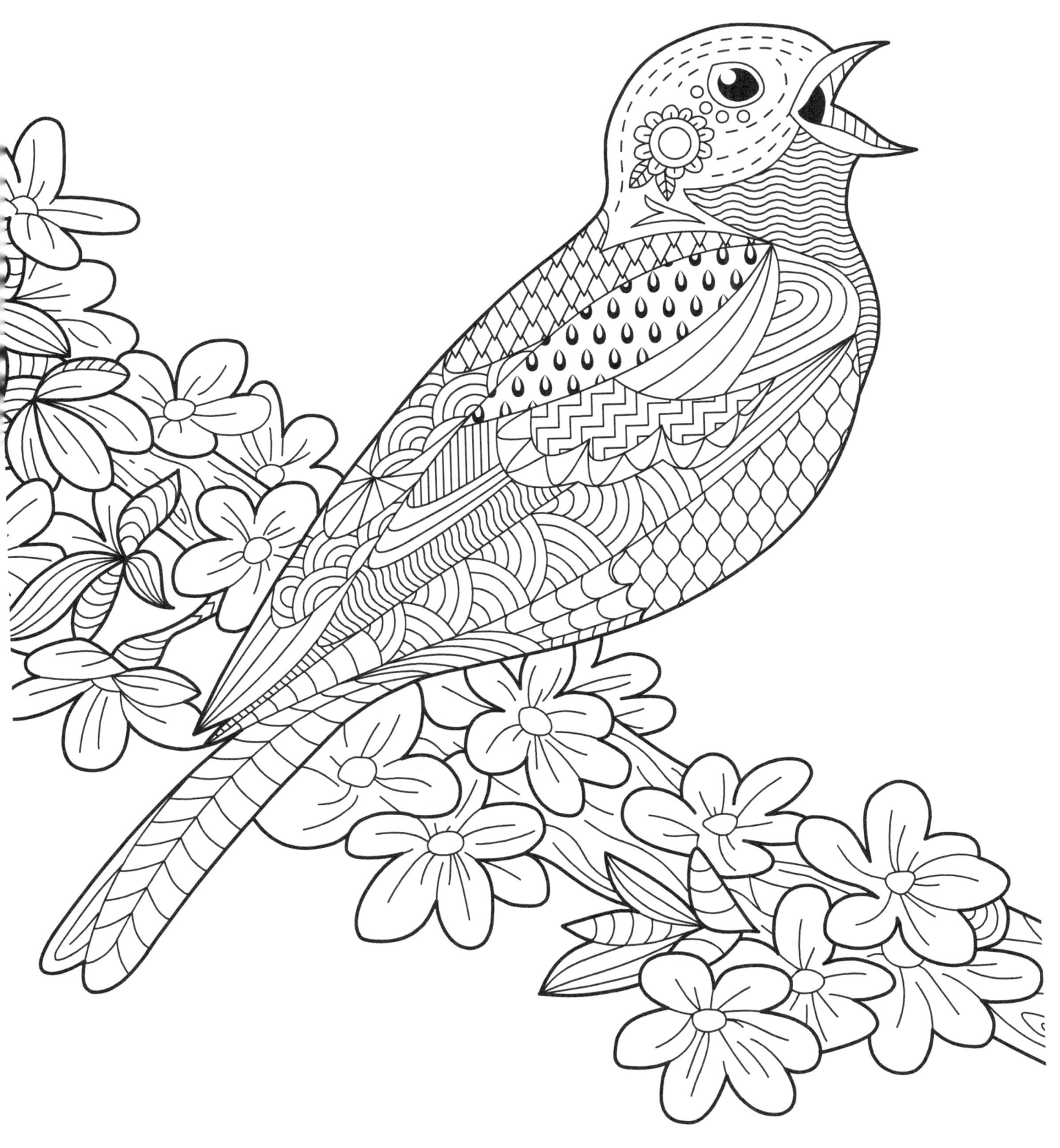

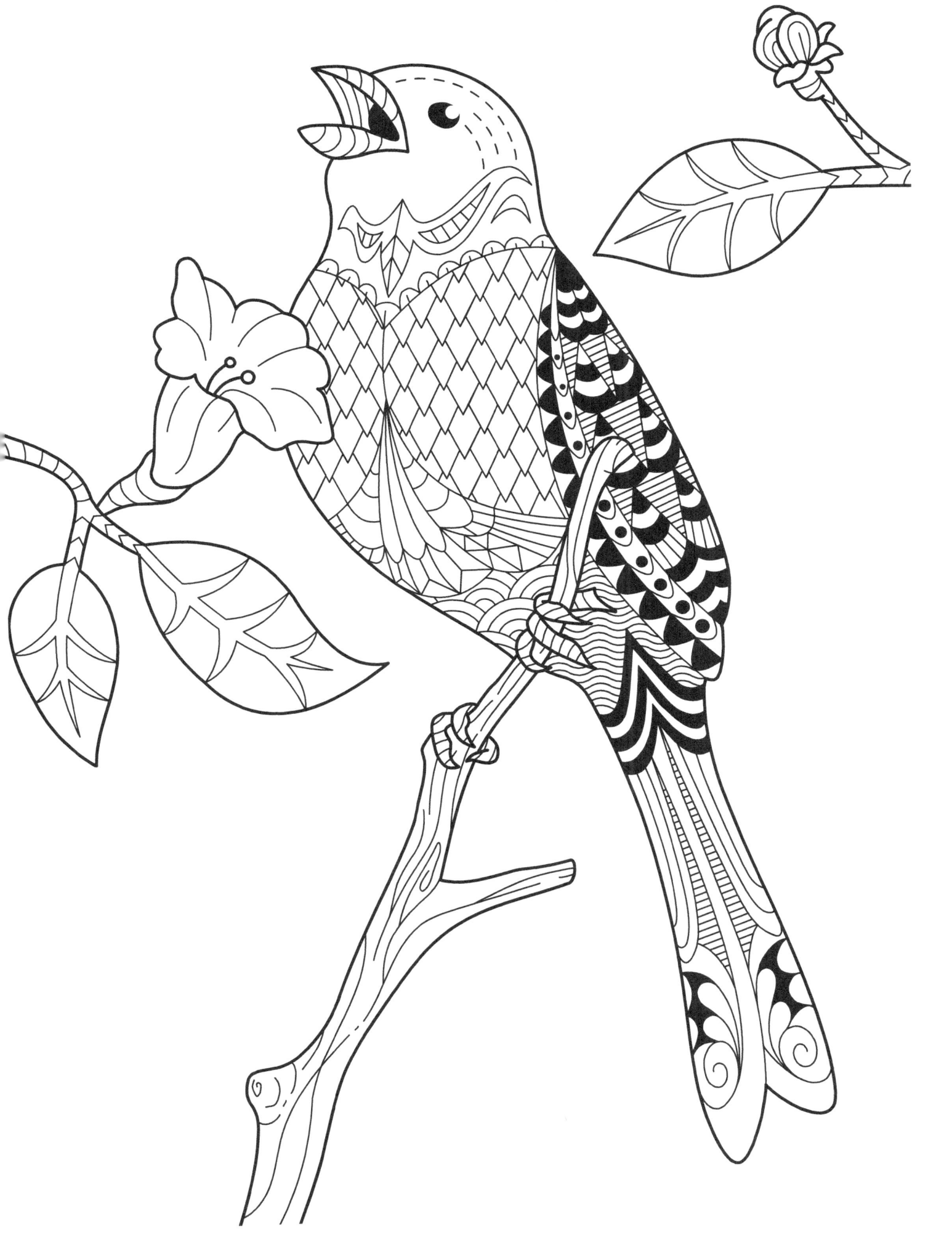

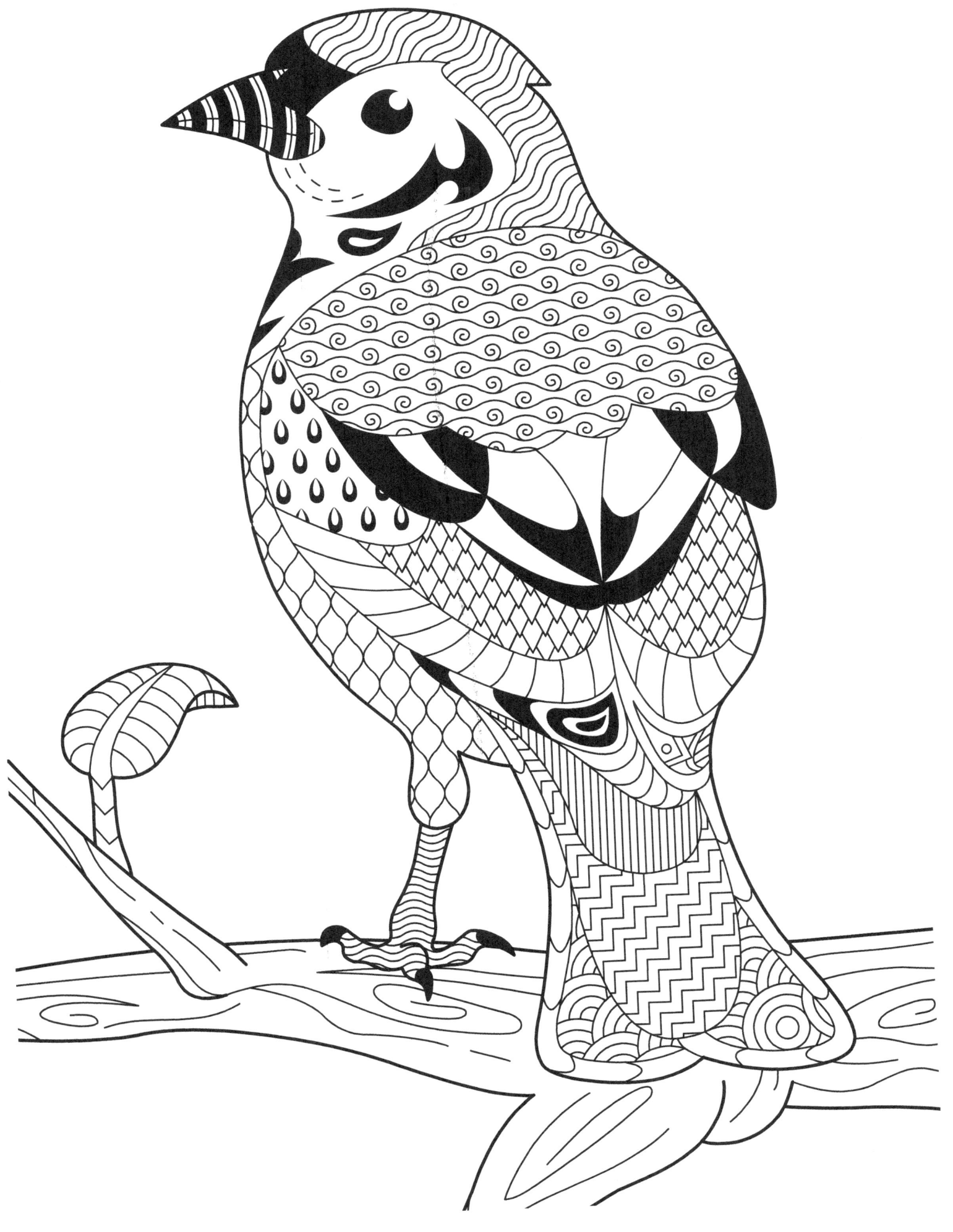

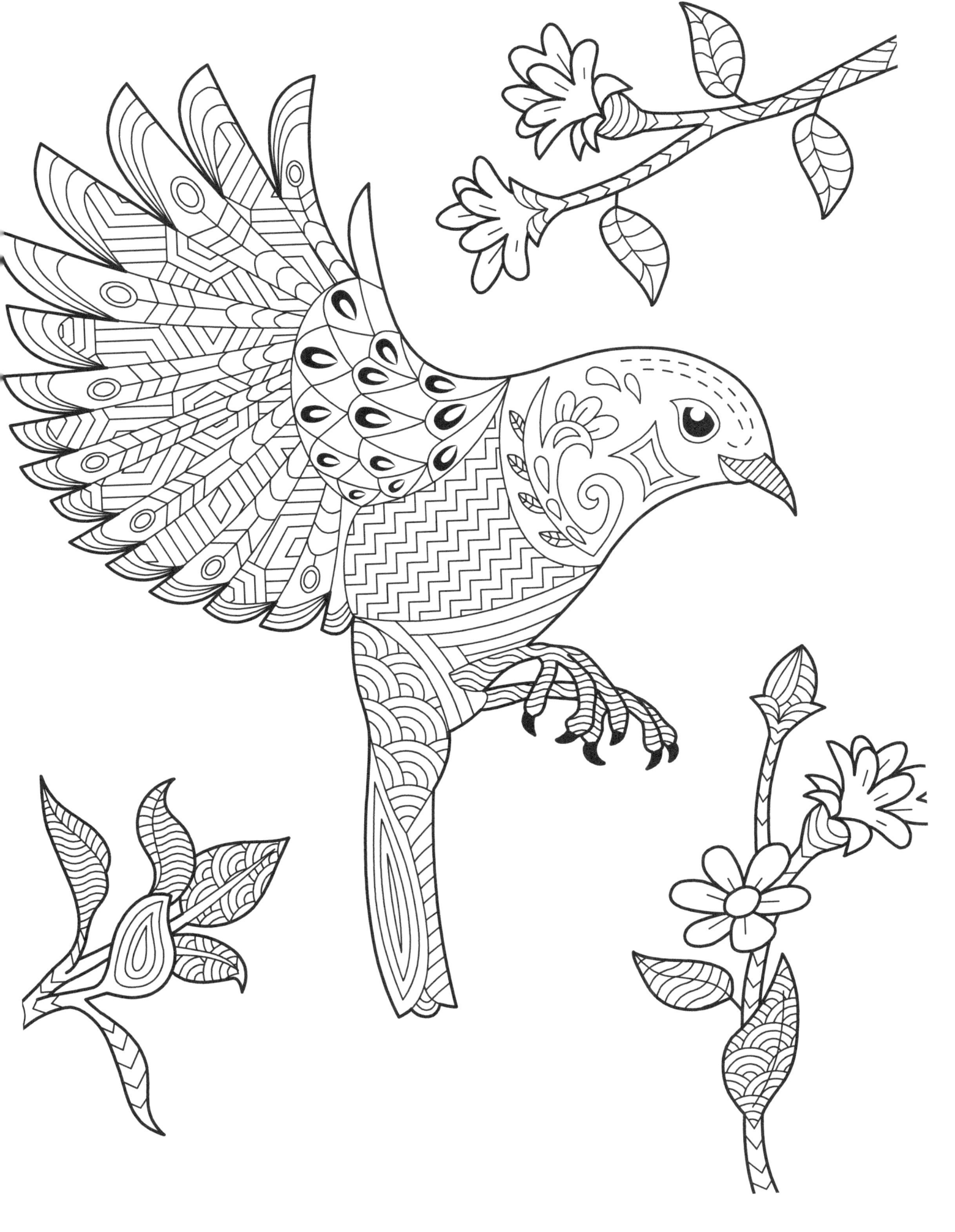

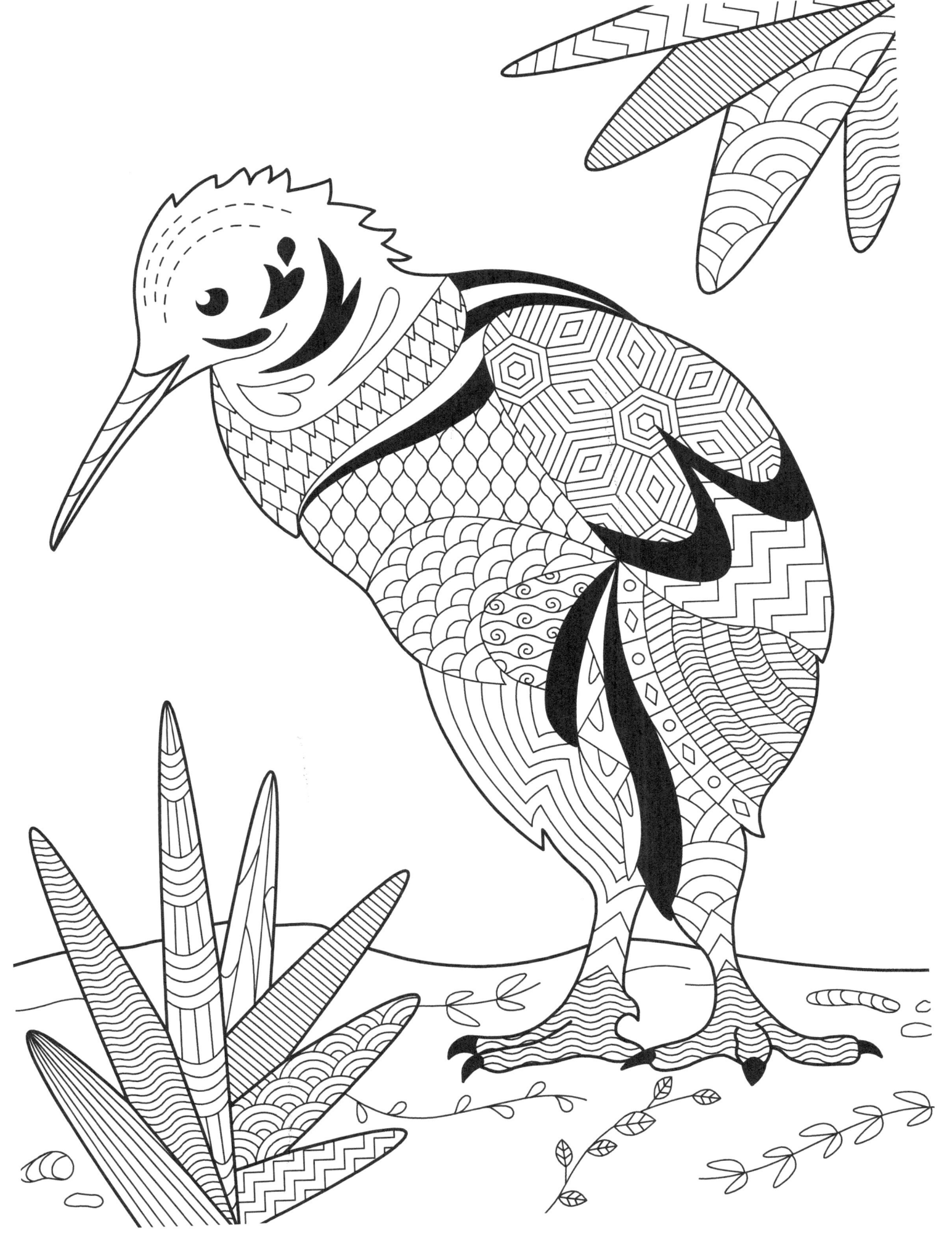

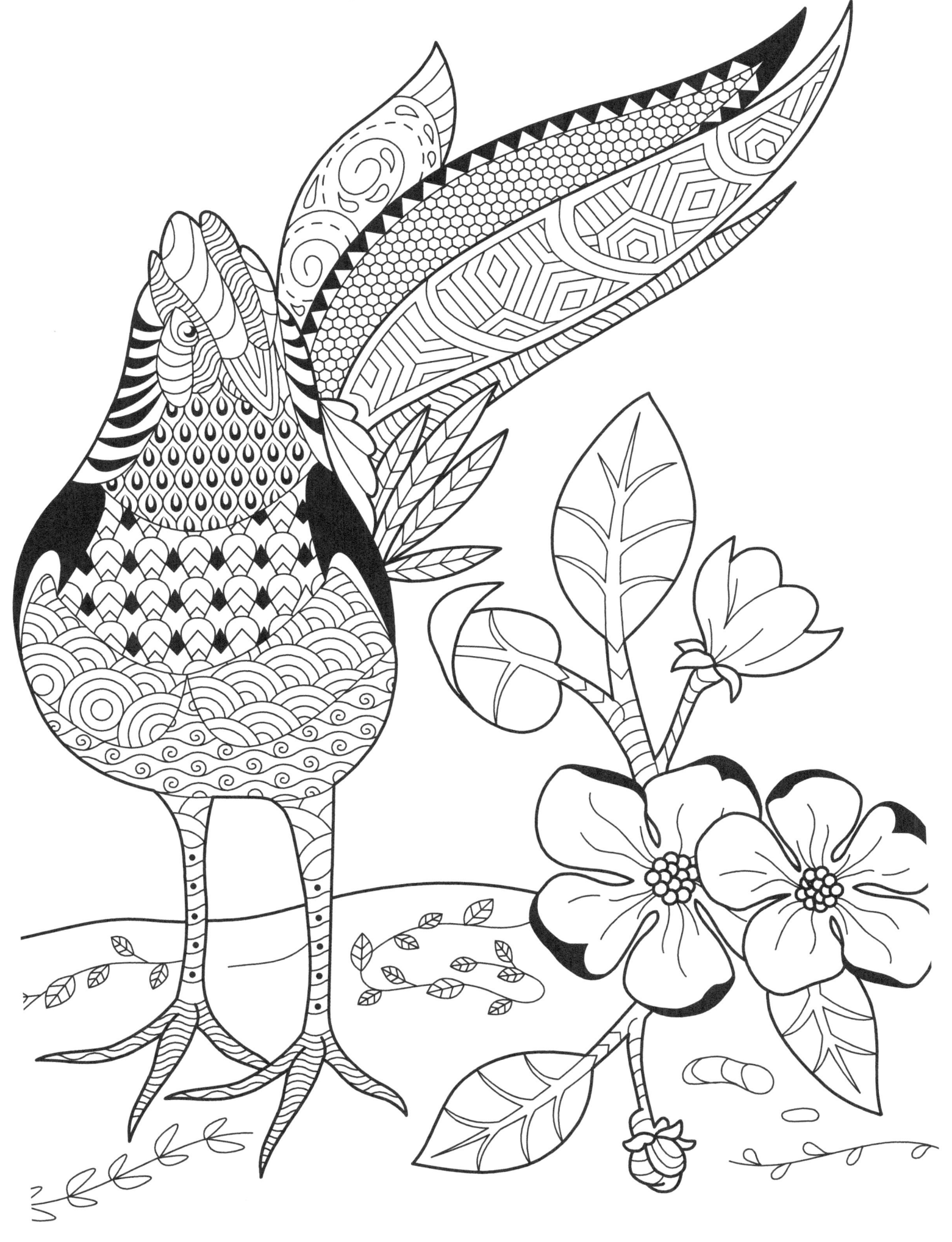

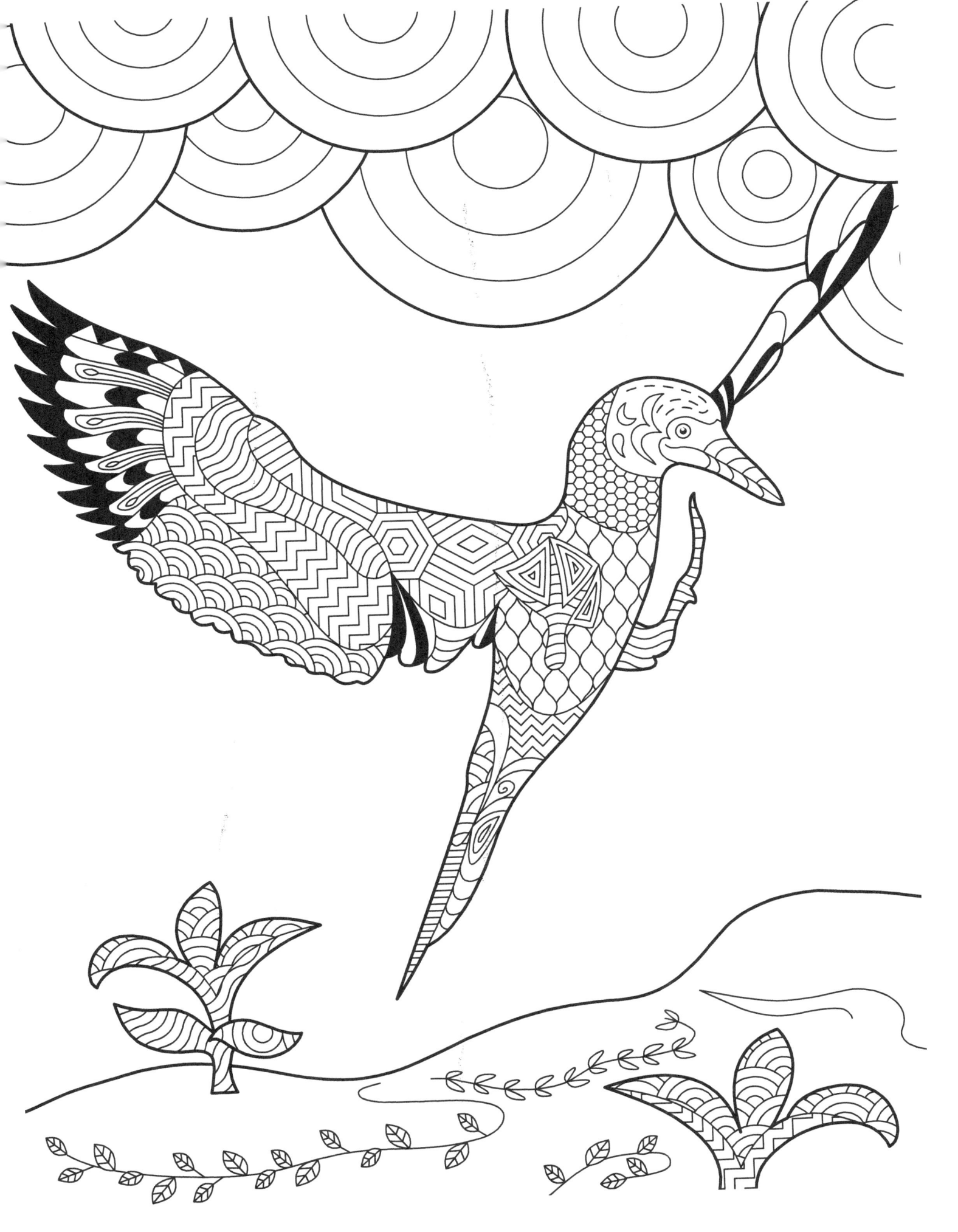

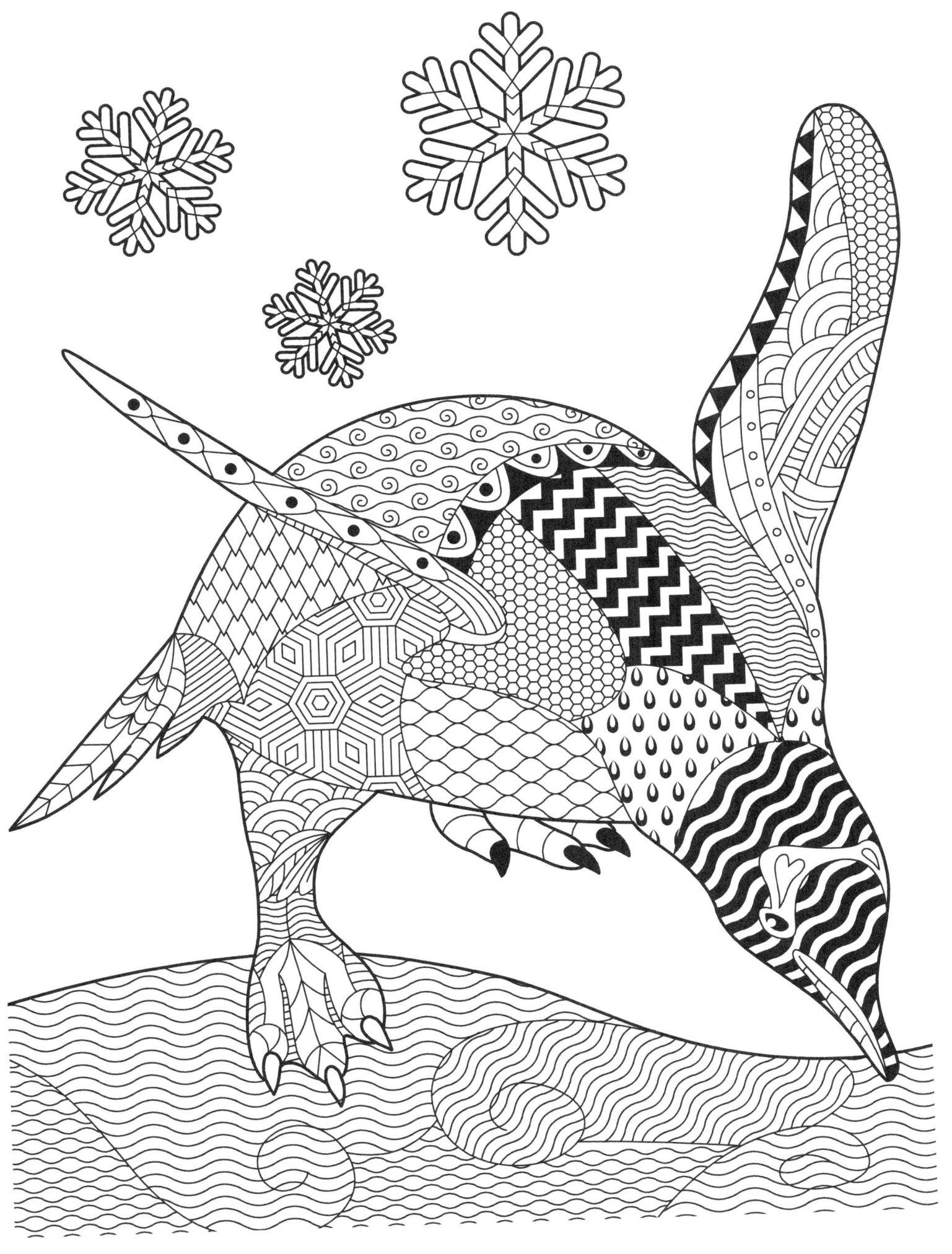

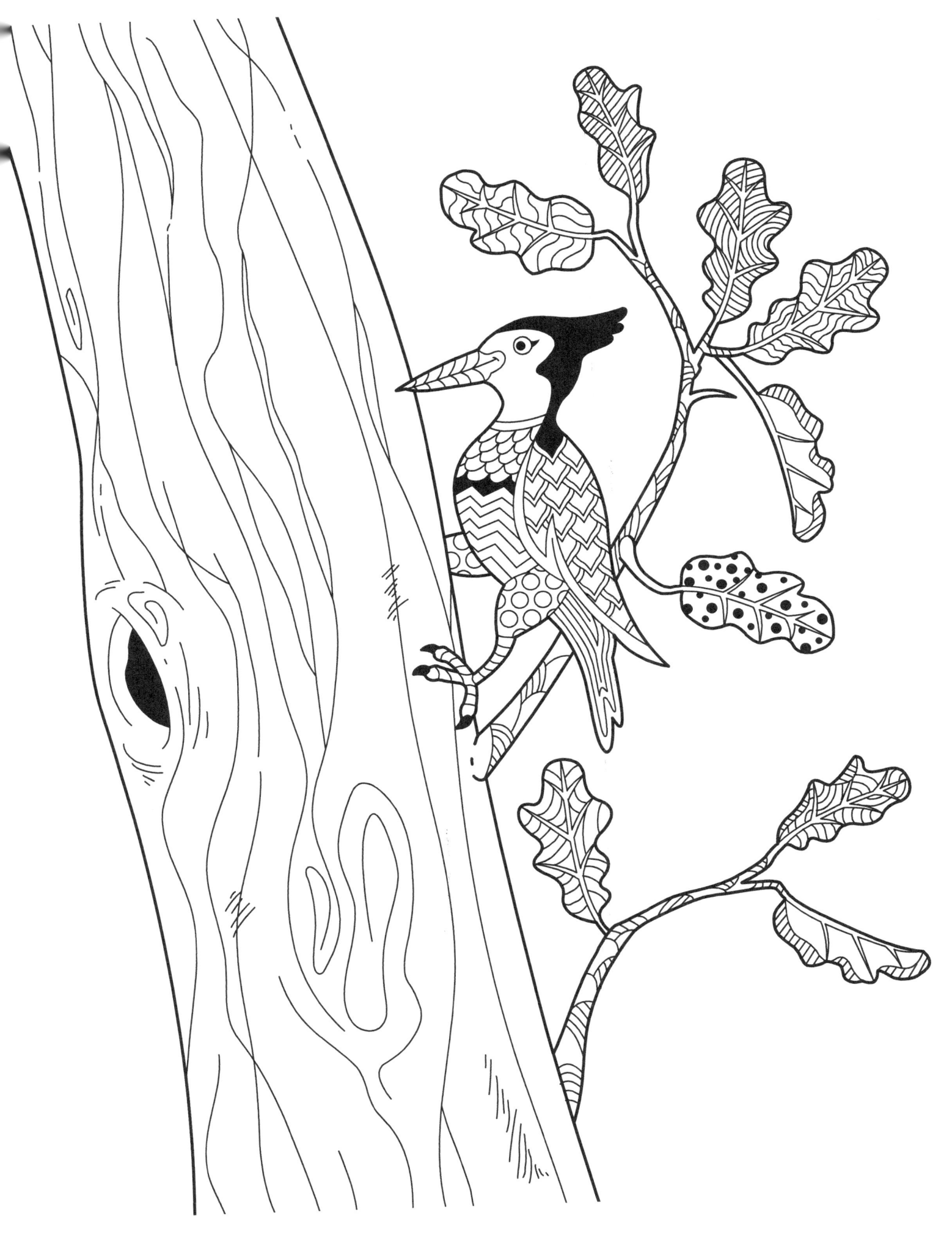

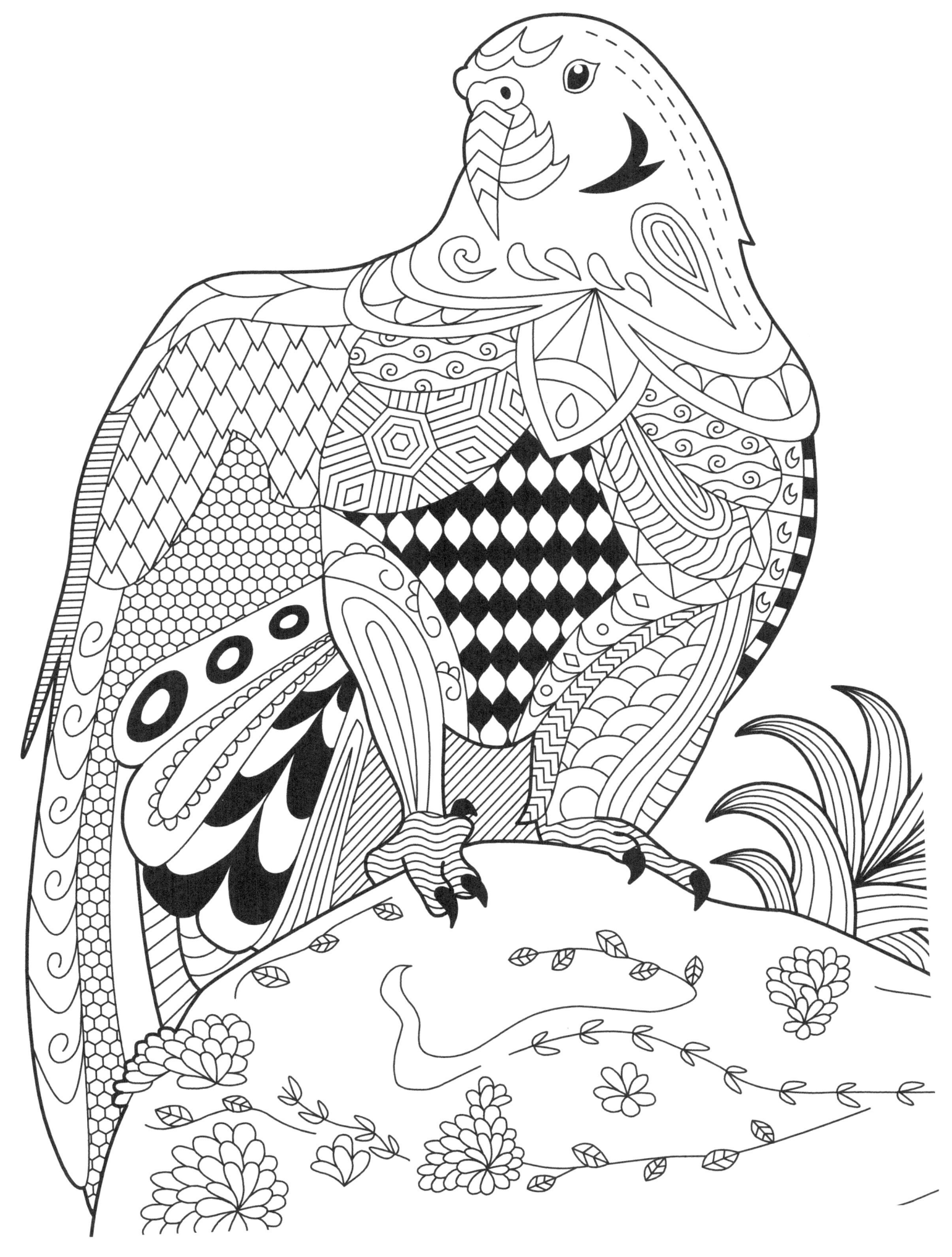

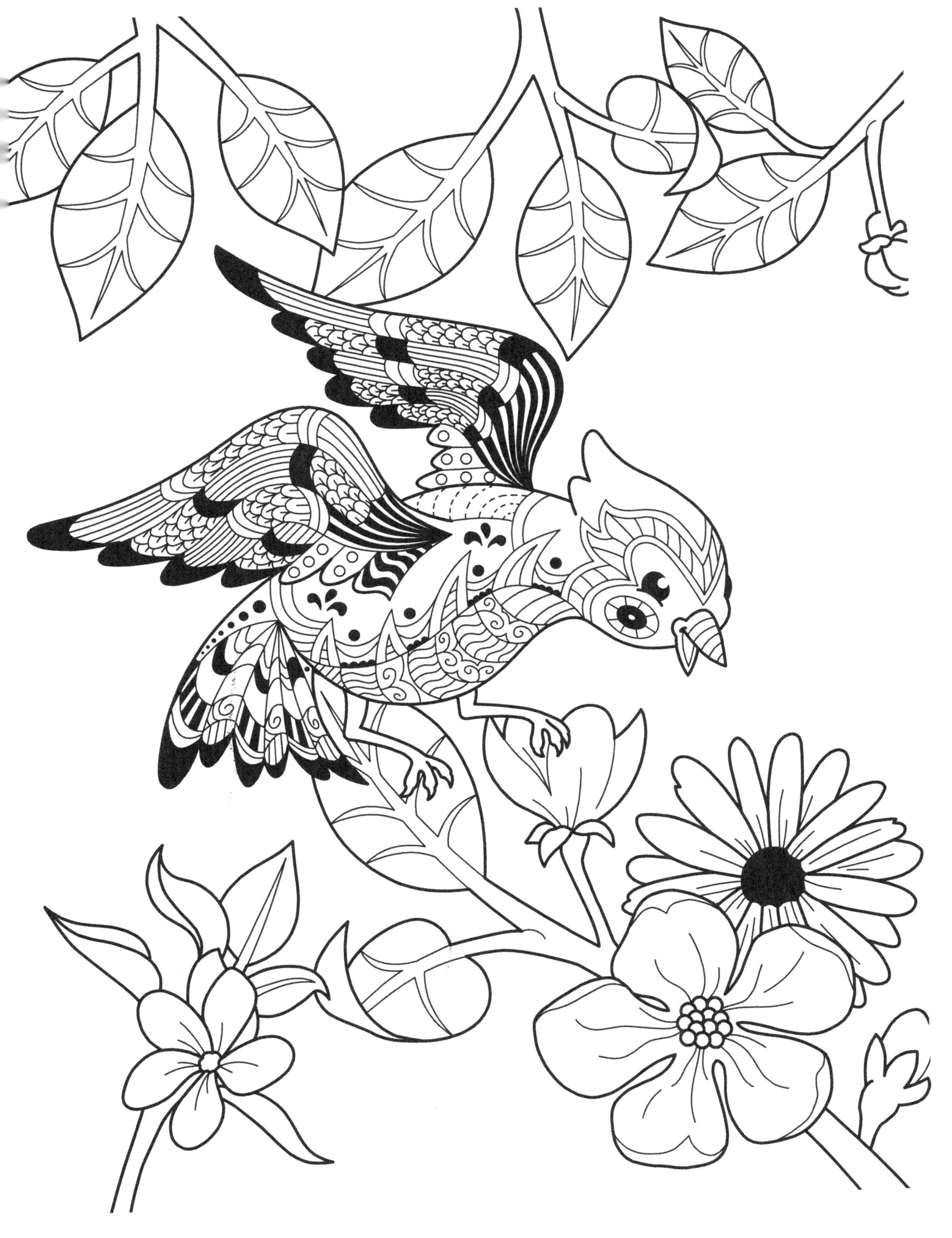

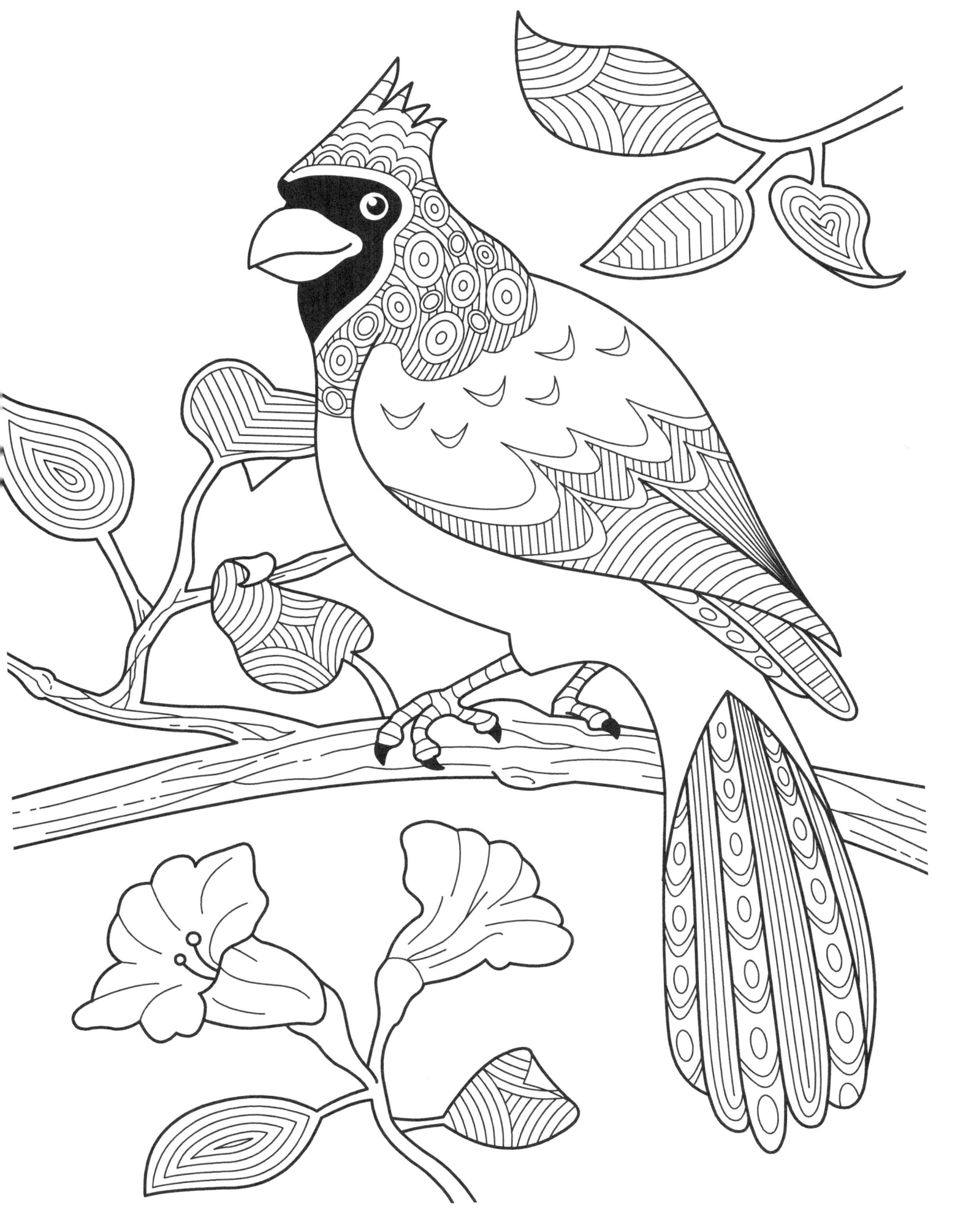

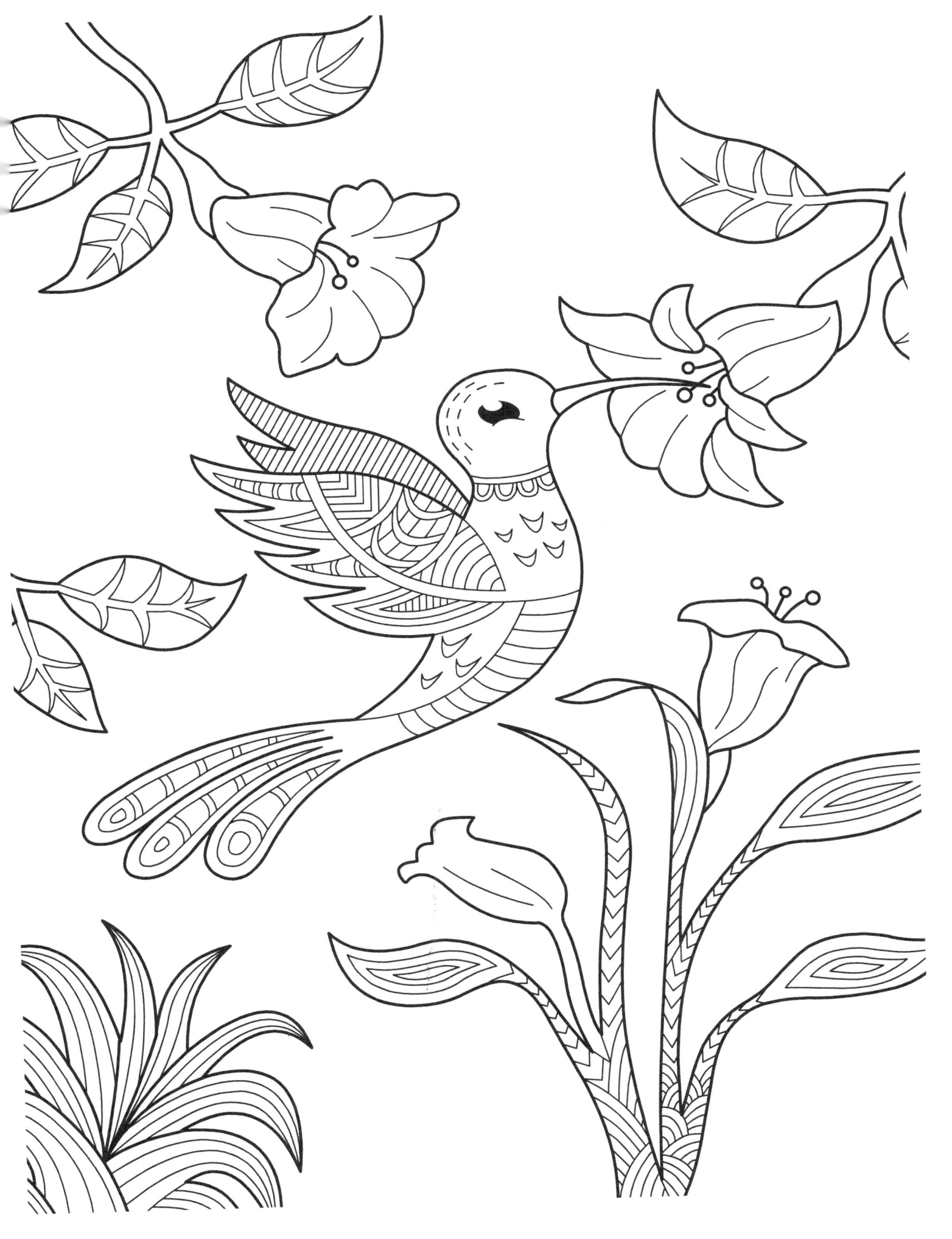

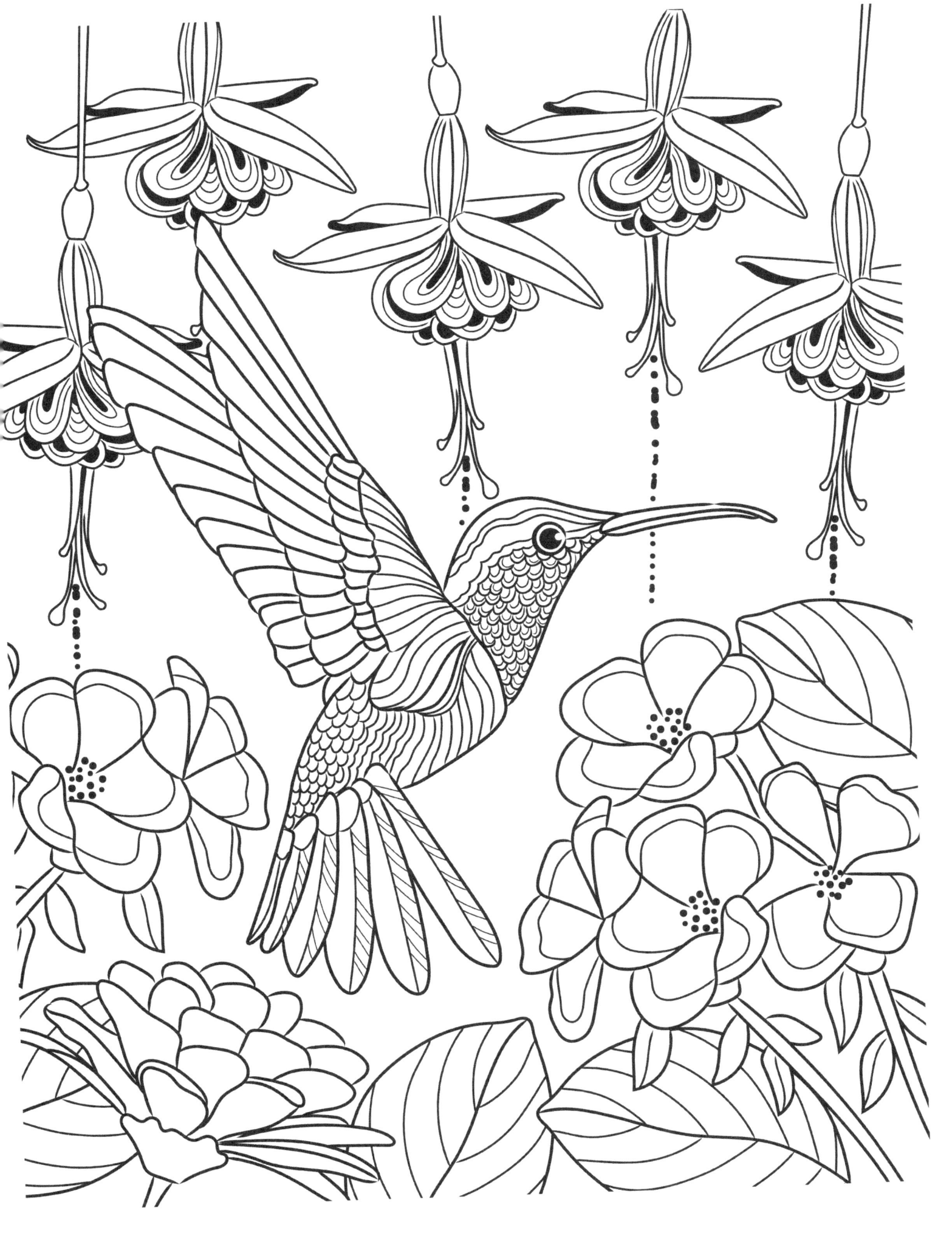

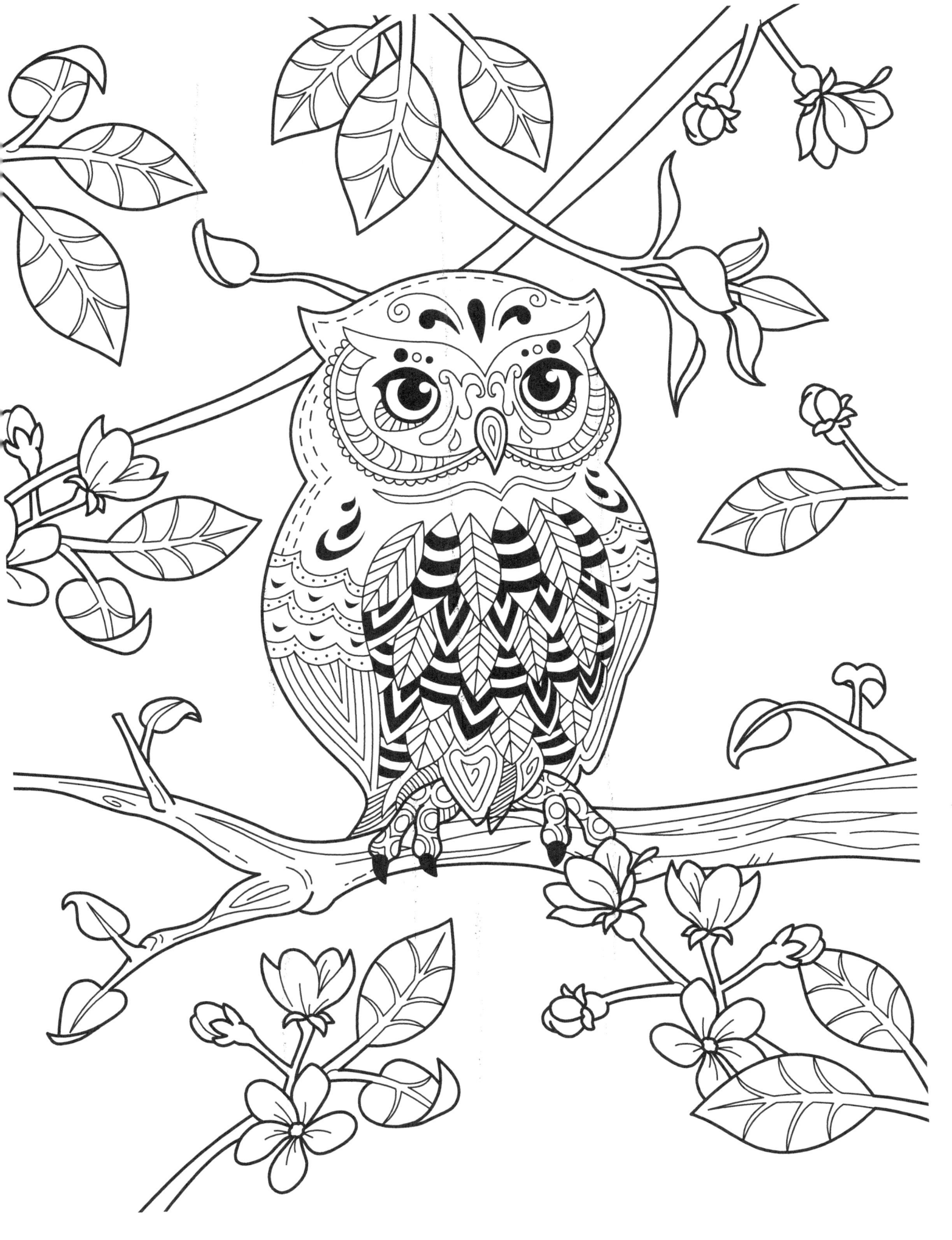

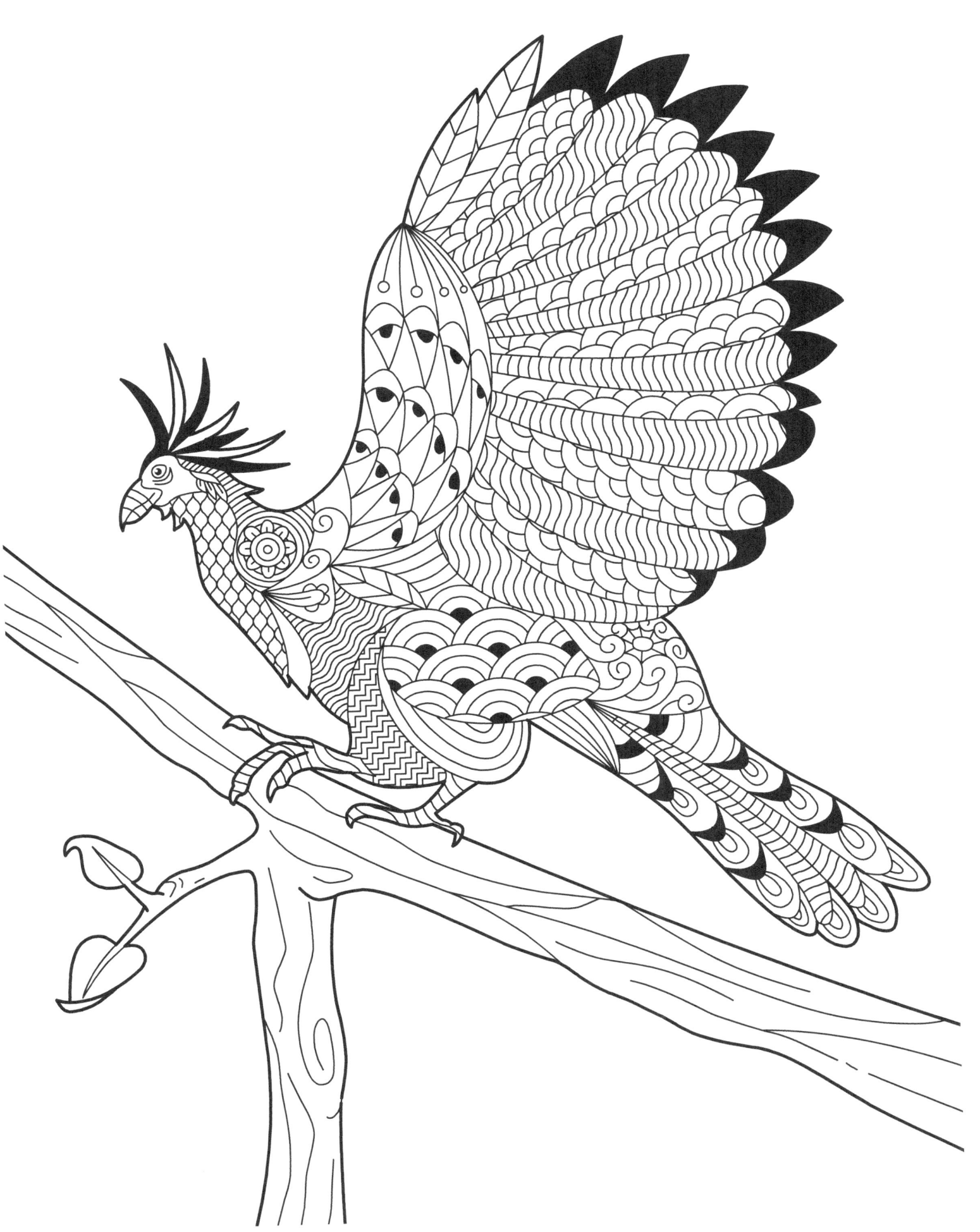

Beautiful Birds & Pretty Patterns

A Bird Nerd Coloring Book Gift

Wow! You made it to the end, we really hope that you enjoyed the book and had many happy hours coloring away!

If you really loved it we would love feedback, and hope that you check out the rest of our range we have to offer!

With love, Veich Publishing.

www.ingramcontent.com/pod-product-compliance
Lightning Source LLC
Chambersburg PA
CBHW080521220526
45465CB00006B/2562